MAD LOVE

A French Modernist Library

Series Editors: Mary Ann Caws,
Richard Howard, Patricia Terry

MAD LOVE

(L'Amour fou)

by André Breton

Translated by Mary Ann Caws

University of Nebraska Press

Lincoln and London

Originally published as *L'Amour fou,*
© Éditions Gallimard, 1937

First Bison Book printing: 1988
Most recent printing indicated
by the first digit below:
        4 5 6 7 8 9 10

Library of Congress Cataloging in
Publication Data
Breton, André, 1896–1966.
Mad love (L'Amour fou)
(A French modernist library)
Bibliography: p.
I. Title: Mad love. II. Series.
PQ2603.R35A813   1986
848'.91207   86-24889
ISBN 0-8032-1200-3 (alk. paper)
ISBN 0-8032-6072-5 (pbk.)

∞

$7.95 MW 8-24-97 (7/2)

M_ad Love_ was written for Jacqueline Lamba, an artist, and the heroine of the night of the Sunflower, whose singular and mysterious beauty, whose intensity of character marks the address of its pages. In the name Aube, the daughter born of André Breton and Jacqueline, and to whom the last letter is dedicated, in this name of Dawn, there is suggested a whole day, opening out from its pages into some other space.

Contents

I should like my life to leave after it no
other murmur than that of the watchman, a song
to while away the waiting. — *Mad Love,* p. 33

Translator's **I***ntroduction*

Breton and the Background

Founder of the surrealist movement,
André Breton (born in Tinchebray in the Orne, in 1896) was one
of the twentieth century's great writers. His highly poetic prose,
even more than his poems, bears witness to a magnetic power of
language and an unsurpassed lyric imagination. *Mad Love* of 1937
is his masterpiece, an incandescent testimony to the love of the
irrational and the irrational of love.[1]

Before this date, he had, during the war, served in various neuro-
psychiatric centers, been associated briefly with the Dada group in
Paris (Tristan Tzara, Paul Eluard, and others),[2] and had experi-
mented widely with "automatic" writing and sleep hypnosis, according to the surrealist advocacy of the liberation of the unconscious
through such means. He had been associated with the presurrealist
journal *Littérature* in 1919 (ironically titled, for one of its other or
under-meanings is *Lis tes ratures,* or "read your scrapings"),[3] and
subsequently had been in charge of the surrealist journal *The Surrealist Revolution* (1922), which then became politicized under the

name *Surrealism at the Service of the Revolution* in 1929. Later, he was to run the art journal *Minotaur* (1932); then, during his time in New York, he founded the journal *VVV* in 1944 with Marcel Duchamp, David Hare, and Max Ernst. At the end of his life, he was associated with three further journals, *Médium* (1952), *Surrealism Itself* (1956), and *The Breach: Surrealist Action* (1961).

As important as the journals were the surrealist manifestoes, the *Surrealist Manifesto* of 1924, and then the *Second Surrealist Manifesto* in 1930, which drew certain limits, excluded certain former members (Antonin Artaud and Robert Desnos), and set the tone for the surrealism of the 1930s.

At the time Breton wrote *Mad Love,* he had already written the autobiographical document *Nadja* (1928), the theoretical tract *The Communicating Vessels* (1932), and several volumes of poetry, including *The White-Haired Revolver* (1932) and *The Air of Water* (1934), poems at once odd and brilliant.[4]

After writing *Mad Love,* he traveled with *Mad Love*'s heroine, the artist Jacqueline Lamba, to Mexico, where with Leon Trotsky he founded the International Federation of Independent Revolutionary Art. In 1938 he wrote the tract "Ni de votre guerre ni de votre paix." In 1939 Breton was drafted in Poitiers; then he and Lamba went to Marseilles, where Breton wrote a long poem, *Fata Morgana* (1940); from there they sailed for New York, where he was a speaker for the Voice of America and was closely linked to the New York art scene. Lamba left Breton and, at the time of this writing, continues to paint in Paris. Their daughter, Aube, was born in Paris in 1935.

Breton married Elisa Bindhoff in 1945; wrote for her in that year *Arcane 17*, set in the Gaspé peninsula; visited the American Southwest (writing the *Ode to Charles Fourier* there in 1945) and Haiti; and then returned to Paris in 1946.

In 1953, he published a group of essays, *The Key to the Fields*. In 1955, *Prolegomena to a Third Manifesto or Not* continued the propagation of surrealist ideas, even as they had been changed by time, thus keeping "Surrealism Alive in Its Works." He died in 1966 at St.-Cirq-la-Popie, where he and his friends had gathered every summer.

Surrealist Transformation

"Transform the world," said Karl Marx. "Change life," said Arthur Rimbaud. Those were one integral goal for Breton. Rimbaud's celebrated "alchemy of the word"—the making into gold of the ordinary dross of human existence by the magic transformative power of language—was taken over by surrealism and enlarged into the hope of remaking all of existence by the unleashing of hidden resources of creative energy. The attitude advocated by surrealism was at once positive and interrogative: instead of what Breton called "miserabilism," surrealism was always to choose the meliorative instinct of optimistic and poetic belief.

Surrealism is, then, by the vision of Breton, turned towards a positive future possibility; surrealist sight insists—with the Zen master Bashō—that our metaphors be rightly viewed. For example, instead of removing the wings from a dragonfly to call it a red pepper, in a subtractive or reductive move, we should affix wings to the red pepper, in an additive or augmentative mood, to have it become that dragonfly. The attitude is characteristic of the entire movement, whose comportment Breton repeatedly defined as "lyric."

Now the lyric position insists doubly on freedom and on "the dazzling revenge" of human imagination against what had previously been considered the limits of the human mind. Love has to be remade, like life. It is and longs to be always kept as marvelous, safe from the "nul and void moments" which go to make up an ordinary existence.

Nadja, Breton's mad and thus quite unordinary heroine of his 1928 novel by the same name, is no more adapted to "real" life than were the alchemists, with whom Breton feels such a bond: they aimed at transmuting our own base metal into our highest or golden selves. The impulse towards the arcane (*Arcane 17*) in no way rules out an openness to the simple everyday things; nor does madness invalidate the love of the marvelous, that childlike expectation of the next moment, the "disponibilité," or openness to chance, which infuses surrealist writing and thinking at its best.

Breton knew, of course, that dailiness and hardship count in real lives; it is in the face of them that art must hold good, "for the problem is no longer, as it used to be, whether a canvas can hold its own in a wheat field,[5] but whether it can stand up against the daily paper, open or closed, which is a jungle." Art has to stand against famine, against reality, and against what people have done and thought.

Surrealism as Breton conceived it was directed against habit and against the predictable: the famous experiments in automatic writing, made to unleash the dam of the imagination (as the surrealist manifestoes repeatedly point out), provocatively worked towards this end, as did the images in the poems, so upsetting to "normal" ways of seeing. But always the style and the vision of Breton went far past the limits of any experiment, and worked together—as he put it—"to prevent the paths of desire from being overgrown."

The paths of desire and those of writing merge strangely in "automatic" texts such as the poem "Sunflower." Breton claims that the written text cannot be seen in its fullest significance until long after it has moved from writing into life. Thus, the changes he makes in the poem (which is included in *Mad Love*) in order to make it more agreeable are seen by him retrospectively, once the predictive elements are realized, to be errors in vision and not esthetic improvements: the text has its own importance and meaning and must not be altered for trivial or surface considerations.

Even when, later in his life, Breton acknowledges automatic writing to have been a catastrophe, the lesson of *verbal excitement* remains for us. The adherents of surrealism were enthusiasts about the relation of writing and life and chance: they were great writers and great riskers.

Mad Love and Its Book

Mad Love is at once the summation of an *ars poetica* of love and an autobiographical reminiscence about Breton's involvement with Jacqueline Lamba. Like all the great monuments of surrealism, it expresses the entire power and hope of surrealism to remake the world through the emotions and through the confidence that the relation between the exterior or natural world and the interior or human world can reveal more about both than the rational mind could possibly detect. At some moments, this relation takes on a political aura, at others, a purely personal one, and at still others, a mystical one; but the basic confidence remains identical.

Believing that we can remake the world by our thinking and our language, Breton was able to persuade a whole generation of thinkers, writers, and artists to pay attention to their inner gifts and intuitions. They could be seen not only to respond to the world outside but even to discover, in that world, an answer to a question they "were not conscious of having." By what Breton was to call the law of objective chance, he expected the inner and the outer experiences to mingle in an ongoing, constant communion he compared to the scientific experiments of communicating vessels—in which communing opposites merge. Thus the extremes of day and night, up and down, life and death, are held in balance, providing an extraordinary dynamism of activated images, transforming by this vital interchange the deadly dullness of "the unacceptable human condition."

In his own works, Breton stresses the overwhelming power and frightening effect of surrealist love as it participates in the arational marvelous. If the sense of wonder toward the future and toward the state of expectation itself seems overly optimistic, we have only to remember the magnificently doubting passage set in Les Halles at midnight, as the new couple walks among the garbage peelings in the streets of the marketplace at midnight, wondering whether it is not too late to turn back. Here the poet and lover take precedence over the theory writer, and the problematic present weighs more in the balance than the prediction of future events.

Yet in fact the sense of prediction hangs beautiful and heavy over this book—together with an inescapable accent on the tensions between the same and the different. The remarkable and peculiar scene on which it opens relates to this tension: all the beings Breton has loved and the past images of himself corresponding to them are seated on facing benches, as if in judgment. If they are all to be seen as predictive figurations of the final one, then the latter is seen as ultimate and justifies the others. If, on the other hand, they are all separate, no link binds one moment of sentiment to the next, and the game of continuity is surely lost. "Across the diversity of these inconceivable flowers over there, it is you over there changing whom I love in a red blouse, naked, in a gray blouse" (*Mad Love*, p. 81).

The present volume is of unsurpassed importance both within surrealism and to all readers of the surrealist movement. Of all the notions we retain from the heroic period of surrealism, that of "mad love" is primary. It returns to the great medieval tradition of courtly love, on all counts opposed to domestic safeness, being governed by its own rules and reason and not by the ordinary rationality of what it conceives of as a duller state of things, always called by Breton – in his most scornful tone – "bourgeois reason." Romanticism picked up, of course, on that tradition, as does surrealist love, which chooses to inscribe itself in the same lines. It is a line of great and meaningful risk and, in that direction, wills itself revolutionary: thus the "mad" or unreasonable and antisocial character, which was such a crucial part of its project, madder than it was courtly.[6] Mad love is not to be separated into two parts, with the "madness" split from the love, for the intertwining of the former with the latter is what makes the latter distinct.[7] Other surrealists had other modes, to be sure, such as Benjamin Péret's *amour sublime*.[8] The "mad" of Breton's phrasing is strongly related to his own sentimental history, now part of literature and its own history, that of his involvement with the mad Nadja, and of the volume previously translated under that title. Nadja was hopelessly, wonderfully mad, yet alas, as Breton points out within those pages, she was also likely to bore him. Therein lies the drama, if not from all points of view tragic, at least notable: that the founder of a movement which willed itself the celebrator of what was most mad and most undomesticated should have rejected, finally, a woman not just mad for love, but really mad. "They came," reads one notable sentence in the book, "to tell me Nadja was insane." Her casting out from the surrealist mode made her fame within surrealist history for those who read it now, even as it sheds an ironic light upon the very idea of what can be accepted about the unacceptable, and vice versa.

This book, however, picks up love where it was left, picks it up after X, the woman turned to after the actual madwoman Nadja, and resurrects at once the sense of its high and grand insanity and the sense of its redemption of all the rest, of all the frittered days and things of ordinary life. *Mad Love* is a book written on a high, and with its lows, its doubts, always and necessarily a part of this love so intense as not to be able to endure except variously. It preserves what it celebrates, and preserves it in its very unevenness.

The object itself, the book *Mad Love,* was originally an object-book, in the classic surrealist style, interleaved with photographs, by Cartier-Bresson, Brassaï, and Man Ray,[9] and with letters from Breton stuck between the pages. It bears witness to the encounter between the vision and the world, the word and the objects, the producer of objects and of signs and the reader of both, then and now. It proves its own startling kind of existence in the real world, being not just a book, not just the record of an extraordinary love – that between André Breton and the artist with whom he shared his life – but an object inserted madly and really, now in our world. The objects within the book, as they are photographed and *kept,* exist in the same odd space as the book-object, but also on an inner level, as if within the mise-en-abyme, the one-in-the-other insertion towards infinity.

Translating Difficulties

L'Amour fou proves itself singularly difficult to translate, being at once lyric and vaguely – sometimes desperately – stilted; at once romantic and classical, it contains the essence of surrealism itself in its highest and most idiosyncratic style. As in the recent volume *Difference in Translation,*[10] where a group of critics work out the notion of "translation effects," stressing the ambivalence of such effects on the understanding of both original and rendering, it is above all a question of pressure points with all their tension. Here a singleness of expression turns doubly or triply on an enlargement of meaning behind the single sense.

In particular, in the translation here, it is not a question of being "right" or "wrong," or then "faithful" or "fickle" – rather, more of trying to express the ongoing and deep relation of the translation to the original, they being complementary in nature as if they were signifying fragments of some larger whole. The translation may be seen turning like the sunflower, its emblematic incarnation, toward the captivating and terrible illumination of Breton's prose and yet placing itself in doubt in relation to the original effect of the French text, totally unlike other texts as it is. This is, it seems to me, the only original worth *going after,* the one we sense behind what we read; to go after it is not to chase a prey for complete capture, but to believe in an interior and impulsive correspondence with one of the truest surrealist texts.

To translate such a classic in the sure knowledge of failure is – perhaps – to make an impossible gesture of gratitude to a work and an author of primary significance for us all. It is really a gesture, all these years later, of our own mad love.

My warmest thanks to Micheline Tison-Braun for her constant and wise advice in this translation, to Isabelle Lorenz for her enthusiastic help, and to Carole Kulikowski for her patience and support. For the spontaneity with which Geoffrey Harris offered a last-minute rereading of the first chapters, I am deeply grateful.

M.A.C., NEW YORK, JANUARY 1987

MAD LOVE

for Jacqueline **L**amba, *this translation*

1 *Boys* of harsh discipline, nameless actors, chained and brilliant, from the grand musical that will always occupy the mental theatre, with no hope for change, have always mysteriously evoked for me certain theoretical beings, whom I interpret as key-bearers, possessing the *clues to situations.*[1] I mean that they hold the secret of the most meaningful attitudes I shall have to take in the presence of some rare events which will have left their mark upon me.[2] These characters habitually appear to me dressed in black – probably in full dress; their faces escape me, but I think there are seven or so of them, seated next to each other on a bench, talking among themselves, always looking straight ahead. That is the way I should have liked to put them on stage in the play's opening scene, their role being to unveil, with a certain cynicism, the motives for the action. At nightfall and often much later (I know perfectly well that psychoanalysis would have something to say about this), as if they were submitting to a ritual, I find them wandering speechless by the sea, in single file, winding lightly around the waves. Coming from them, this silence is no hardship, their conversation on that bench always having seemed to me, to tell the truth, singularly disconnected. If I were to try to find an antecedent in literature for them, I might well come up with Jarry's *Haldernablou,* where a litigious language like theirs flows easily, with no immediate exchange value, *Haldernablou,* which also ends with an evocation very close to my own: "in the triangular forest after dusk."[3]

Why must this phantasm be irresistibly followed by another one, obviously located at the antipodes of the first? In the construction of the ideal play I was speaking of, it manages to have the final curtain fall upon an episode that is lost backstage, or is at least played out on this stage at an uncommon depth. Some imperious concern for equilibrium is in control here, opposing, from one day to the next, any variation. The rest of the play is a matter of caprice – that is, as I immediately tend to understand it, it is scarcely worth dreaming up. I like to imagine all the enlightenment that the spectator will have enjoyed converging in this *shadowy point*. Oh what a praiseworthy grasp of the problem, what good-hearted laughter and tears, a human taste for accepting or rejecting: what temperate climes! But suddenly, perhaps again the bench we just saw, it doesn't matter, or some café bench, the scene is blocked off once more. Blocked off, this time, by a row of seated women in pale clothes, the most appealing they have ever worn. Symmetry dictates they must be seven or nine. A man enters. . . and recognizes them: one after the other, all at once? They are the women he has loved, who have loved him, some for years, others for one day. How dark it is!

It's because I'm absolutely forbidden to imagine, in such a case, the behavior of any man at all—as long as he is a coward—this man in whose place I have so often been, that I can't think of anything more pathetic. He scarcely *is* at all, this living man who would hoist himself up on this treacherous trapeze of time. He would be unable even to exist without forgetfulness, that ferocious beast with its larva-like features. The wonderful little diamond slipper was heading off in several directions.[4]

We must try to glide, not too quickly, between the two impossible tribunals facing each other: the first, of the lovers I shall have been, for example; the other, of these women I see, all in pale clothes. So the same river swirls, snatches, sheds its veils, and runs by, under the spell of the sweetness of the stones, the shadows, and the grasses. The water, mad for its swirls like a real mane of fire. To glide like water into pure sparkle—for that we would have to have lost the notion of time. But what defense is there against it; who will teach us to decant the joy of memory?

History does not say that romantic poets, although they have composed for themselves a less dramatic conception of love than ours, have succeeded in confronting the storm. On the contrary, the examples of Shelley, Nerval, Arnim, illustrate in a striking way the conflict which will be progressively more bitter until our time, for the mind chooses to believe that the loved object is a *unique* being, whereas often social conditions of life can destroy such an illusion. This largely explains, I believe, the feeling of malediction weighing on man today and expressing itself so acutely through the most characteristic works of this last century.

Making due allowance for the use of any means needed to transform the world and notably to suppress these social obstacles, it is nevertheless perhaps not useless to persuade ourselves that this idea of a unique love comes from a mystic attitude—which doesn't mean it can't be nourished by contemporary society for its own dubious ends. All the same I think I see a possible synthesis of this idea and its negation. It is not, in fact, just the parallel lineup of these two rows of men and women I was just pretending to see earlier as equals, that persuades me how likely it is that the man in question—in all these faces of men called up in which he finally recognizes only himself—will discover at the same time in all these women's faces one face only: the *last* face loved. How many times, moreover, have I noticed that under extremely dissimilar appearances one exceptional trait was developing, and one attitude that I might have thought taken from me forever. However distressing such an hypothesis remains for me, it could be that in this domain, substituting one person for another or even several others, tends towards an always clearer definition of the physical aspect of the beloved, through the always increasing subjectivization of desire. The beloved would then be the one in whom would mingle a certain number of particular qualities considered more appealing than the others and appreciated separately, successively, in all the beings loved to some extent previously. This proposition corroborates in a dogmatic form the popular notion of the "type" of woman or man or of the individual man or woman considered alone. I am saying that here as elsewhere this notion, being the fruit of a collective judgement tried and proved, appears fortunately to correct another one emerging from one of those innumerable idealistic pretensions which have proved themselves intolerable in the long run.

And it is there—right in the depths of the human crucible, in this paradoxical region where the fusion of two beings who have really chosen each other renders to all things the lost colors of the times of ancient suns, where however, loneliness rages also, in one of nature's fantasies which, around the Alaskan craters, demands that under the ashes there remain snow—it is there that years ago I asked that we look for a new beauty, a beauty "envisaged exclusively to produce passion."[5] I confess without the slightest embarrassment my profound insensitivity in the presence of natural spectacles and of those works of art which do not straight off arouse a physical sensation in me, like the feeling of a feathery wind brushing across my temples to produce a real shiver. I could never avoid establishing some relation between this sensation and that of erotic pleasure, finding only a difference of degree. Although I never manage to exhaust by analysis all the elements of this disquiet—it must in fact come from my repressed feelings—all I know of it persuades me that there sexuality alone presides. Naturally, in these conditions, the very special emotion aroused can rise up for me at the most unexpected times and be caused by something or someone not, on the whole, particularly dear to me. It is nonetheless clearly a question of that kind of emotion and not of another: I insist that I cannot be mistaken in this—it is really as if I had been lost and they had come to give me some news about myself. The first time I visited Paul Valéry, when I was seventeen, I remember his insistent questions about my reasons for devoting myself to poetry. I responded already along the same lines: I was only trying, I said to him, to obtain (to procure for myself?) states of mind like those which certain odd poetic movements had aroused in me. It is striking and admirable that such states of perfect receptivity suffer no diminution in time because, among the examples I am now tempted to give of those short formulas having a magic effect on me, several of those I proposed to Valéry more than twenty years ago return. For example, I remember so well "How salubrious a wind!" from Rimbaud's "The River at Cassis,"[6] or "Then, as the night was aging," of Mallarmé from Poe,[7] and perhaps most of all the conclusion of this advice from a mother to her daughter in a story by Louys: to be wary, I think, of the young men going along the road "with the evening wind and winged dust."[8] Need I say that such extremely rare cases, with the discovery some time later of Isidore Ducasse and his *Chants de Maldoror* and his *Poems,* then blossomed into an unexpected profusion? Lautréamont's "Beautiful as a. . ." constitutes the very manifesto of convulsive poetry.[9] Big bright eyes, of dawn or willow, of fern-crozier, of rum or saffron, the most beautiful eyes of museums or of life open wide at their approach as flowers spread open so as to see no longer, upon all the branches of the air. These eyes, expressive beyond all nuance of ecstasy, rage, fear, these are the eyes of Isis ("And the ardor of yesteryear. . ."), the eyes of women fed to the lions, the eyes of Justine and Juliette, of Lewis's Mathilda, of several of Gustave Moreau's faces, of certain contemporary wax effigies.[10] But if Lautréamont reigns without question over the immense country source of most of these irresistible appeals, I shall nonetheless continue to call upon all those whose wording has utterly transfixed me some time or another, placing me entirely under the sway of Baudelaire ("And strange flowers. . ."), of Cros, of Nouveau, of Vaché, less often of Apollinaire, or even of a poet more than forgettable, Michel Féline ("And the postulant virgins . . . Repose for their breasts").[11]

The word "convulsive," which I use to describe the only beauty which should concern us, would lose any meaning in my eyes were it to be conceived in motion and not at the exact expiration of this motion. There can be no beauty at all, as far as I am concerned—convulsive beauty—except at the cost of affirming the reciprocal relations linking the object seen in its motion and in its repose.[12] I regret not having been able to furnish, along with this text, the photograph of a speeding locomotive abandoned for years to the delirium of a virgin forest.[13] Besides wanting to see *that,* which I find particularly exaltating, it seems to me that the most magical aspect of this monument to victory and to disaster would have been that of capturing ideas. Moving from force to fragility, I see myself now in a grotto in the Vaucluse, contemplating a little limestone deposit upon the very dark earth, looking just like an egg in an eggcup. From the ceiling of the grotto, drops fell with regularity against its delicate upper part, of a blinding white. Within that luminosity seemed to dwell the very apotheosis of those wonderful *Prince Rupert's Drops.* It was almost unsettling to watch such a marvel forming. In another grotto, the Grotto of the Fairies near Montpellier, you walk between high quartz walls, your heart stopping a few seconds at the spectacle of this gigantic mineral overlay called "the imperial mantle," whose drapery forever defies that of any statuary, covered with roses by a spotlight's beams so that it became, even in this way, quite as dazzling as the splendid and convulsive cloak made of the infinite repetition of a unique little red feather of a rare bird that the ancient Hawaiian chieftains used to wear.

But it is completely apart from these accidental figurations that I am led to compose a eulogy to crystal.[14] There could be no higher artistic teaching than that of the crystal. The work of art, just like any fragment of human life considered in its deepest meaning, seems to me devoid of value if it does not offer the hardness, the rigidity, the regularity, the luster on every interior and exterior facet, of the crystal. Please understand that this affirmation is constantly and categorically opposed, for me, to everything that attempts, esthetically or morally, to found formal beauty on a willed work of voluntary perfection that humans must desire to do.[15] On the contrary, I have never stopped advocating creation, spontaneous action, insofar as the crystal, nonperfectible by definition, is the perfect example of it. The house where I live, my life, what I write: I dream that all that might appear from far off like these cubes of rock salt look close up.

This dominion of the senses which stretches over all the domains of my mind, residing in a sheaf of light rays within reach, is, I think, fully shared from time to time only by those absolute bouquets formed in the depths by the alcyonaria, the madrepores. Here the inanimate is so close to the animate that the imagination is free to play infinitely with these apparently mineral forms, reproducing their procedure of recognizing a nest, a cluster drawn from a petrifying fountain. After some castle towers three-quarters ruined, rock crystal towers with their summit in the sky and their feet in fog, from one of whose blue and gilt windows there streams the hair of Venus, after these towers, I was saying, a whole garden appears: the giant reseda, the hawthorn whose stem, whose leaves, whose thorns even, are of the very substance of flowers, the fans of frost. If the very place where the "figure"—in the Hegelian sense of the material mechanism of individuality, beyond magnetism[16]—attains its reality is above all the crystal, then in my view the place where

The house where I live, my life, what I write . . . (p.11)
Photograph by Brassaï. © Gilberte Brassaï 1986

it ideally loses this omnipotent reality is the coral, reintegrated as it should be in life, into the dazzling sparkle of the sea. Life, in its constant formation and destruction, seems to me never better framed for the human eye than between the hedges of blue tit-mouses of aragonite and the treasure bridge of Australia's Great Barrier Reef.

To these first two conditions to which convulsive beauty must respond, in the deepest sense of the term, I think it necessary to add a third, which will suffice to fill in any gaps. Such beauty cannot appear except from the poignant feeling of the thing revealed, the integral certainty produced by the emergence of a solution, which, by its very nature, could not come to us along ordinary logical paths. It is a matter—in such a case—of a solution which is always superior, a solution certainly rigorously fitting and yet somehow in excess of the need. The image, such as it is produced in automatic writing, has always constituted for me a perfect example of this. In just such a way, I have wanted to see some very special object constructed in response to some poetic fantasy. This object, in its matter, in its form, I more or less predicted. Now I have chanced to discover it, unique, doubtless, among so many other fabricated objects. It was obviously this one, it always differed in every way from what I had foreseen. You might have said that, in its extreme simplicity, which did not keep it from answering the most complicated needs of the problem, it put the elementary character of my predictions to shame. I shall return to that. In any case, what is delightful here is the dissimilarity itself which exists between the object wished for and *the object found*.[17] This *trouvaille,* whether it be artistic, scientific, philosophic, or as useless as anything, is enough to undo the beauty of everything beside it. In it alone can we recognize the marvelous precipitate

The treasure bridge
of Australia's Great
Barrier Reef (p.13)
Photo N.-Y.-T.

of desire. It alone can enlarge the universe, causing it to relinquish some of its opacity, letting us discover its extraordinary capacities for reserve, proportionate to the innumerable needs of the spirit. Daily life abounds, moreover, in just this sort of small discovery, where there is frequently an element of apparent gratuitousness, very probably a function of our provisional incomprehension, discoveries that seem to me not in the least unimportant. I am profoundly persuaded that any perception registered in the most involuntary way—for example, that of a series of words pronounced off-stage—bears in itself the solution, symbolic or other, of a problem you have with yourself. You only have to know how to get along in the labyrinth. Interpretive delirium begins only when man, ill-prepared, is taken by a sudden fear in the *forest of symbols*.[18] But I maintain that for anyone, watchfulness would do anything rather than pay a second's notice to whatever remains exterior to his desire.

What attracts me in such a manner of seeing is that, as far as the eye can see, it recreates desire. How can you resist the hope of calling forth the beast with miraculous eyes, how can you stand the idea that, sometimes for a long time, it cannot be brought out of its retreat? It's really a question of *charms*. So that, in order to have a woman appear, I have seen myself opening a door, shutting it, opening it again—when I had noticed that it was not enough to slip a thin blade into a book chosen at random, after having postulated that such and such a line on the left page or the right should have informed me more or less indirectly about her dispositions, confirming her immediate arrival or her nonarrival—then starting to displace the objects, setting them in strange positions relative to each other, and so on. This woman did not always come, but then it seems to me, it helped me to understand why she wasn't coming; I seemed to accept her not coming more easily. Other days, when the question of absence, of the invincible lack, was solved, I used to consult my cards, interrogating them far beyond the rules of the game, although according to an invariable personal code, precise enough, trying to obtain from them for now and the future a clear view of my fortune and my misfortune. For years on end, I had always used the same deck, which has on its back the flag of the Hamburg-America Line, and its magnificent motto, "Mein Feld ist die Welt," probably also because in this deck the queen of spades is more beautiful than the queen of hearts. The ways of questioning the deck that I preferred and still prefer supposed from the beginning that you place the cards in a cross, placing in the center what I am asking about: myself and her, love, danger, death, mystery; above, what is hovering; on the left, what can frighten or harm; on the right, what is certain; below, what has been overcome. My impatience at too many evasive answers caused me to interpose, rapidly and within the figure, some central object, highly personalized, such as a letter or a snapshot, which seemed to me to bring better results. This time I alternated two little disturbing characters which I had taken in: a mandrake root, slightly smaller, looking to me like Aeneas carrying his father, and the statuette, in raw rubber, of some strange young person listening, bleeding as I observed, at the slightest scratch with an unstoppable dark sap, a being who particularly touches me insofar as I know neither its origin nor its ends and whom, wrongly or rightly, I have decided to consider as a spell-casting object. Taking into account the rule of probability and any hesitation I might have about it, nothing prevents my declaring that this last object, mediated by my cards, has never told me about anything other than myself, bringing me back always to the living center of my life.

On April 20, 1934, at the height of the "occultation" of Venus

Myself and her (p.16)
Photograph by Man Ray.
© A.D.A.G.P., Paris
V.A.G.A., New York 1986

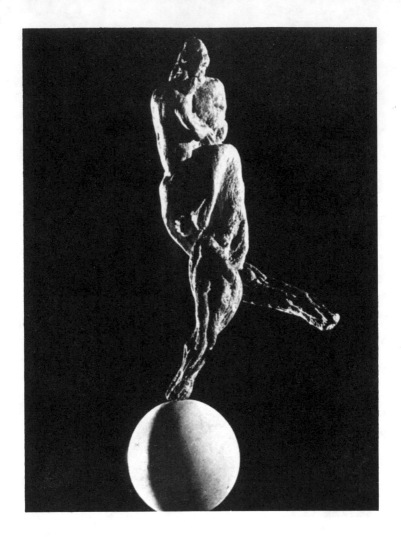

by the moon (this occurrence only supposed to happen once in the year), I was having lunch in a little restaurant rather unfortunately situated near the entrance of a cemetery. To get there, you have to pass in front of a depressing flower display. That day, the sight of a faceless clock on the wall did not seem very tactful. But having nothing better to do, I continued to observe the charming life of the place. In the evening the owner, "who does the cooking," always went home on his motorbike. A few workers appear to be enjoying the cooking. The dishwasher, really good-looking, and evidently quite sharp, sometimes comes out to lean on the counter and discuss apparently serious things with the customers. The waitress is quite pretty: poetic, rather. On April 10 in the morning, she was wearing, over her white collar with red polka dots which harmonized so well with her black dress, a very delicate chain containing three clear drops like moonstones above a crescent of the same material, set in the same way. I again admired the way in which this brooch coincided with the eclipse. As I was trying to situate this young woman, who had been so inspired in this circumstance, the voice of the dishwasher suddenly announced: "Here, l'Ondine!" and the exquisite and childish answer came in a whisper, perfect: "Ah, yes, one dines here!" Could there be a more touching scene? I was still wondering about that in the evening, listening to the actors in the Atelier Theater as they massacred a play by John Ford.

Convulsive beauty will be veiled-erotic, fixed-explosive, magic-circumstantial, or it will not be.

2 "What do you consider the essential encounter of your life? To what extent did this encounter seem to you, and does it seem to you now, to be fortuitous or foreordained?"

Fixed-explosive (p.19)
Photograph by Man Ray.
© A.D.A.G.P., Paris
V.A.G.A., New York 1986

It was in these terms that Paul Eluard and I opened an inquiry whose results the journal Minotaur *printed. At the moment of printing the answers, I felt I had to make more precise the meaning of these two questions as well as to draw some provisional conclusions about the group of opinions that had been expressed.*

If, I wrote, the response to this inquiry (one hundred and forty answers for about three hundred questionnaires sent out) seems quantitatively satisfactory, it would be stretching a point to claim that it had attained all our objectives, and in particular, that the concept of encounter had been brilliantly elucidated. Still, the very nature of the responses sent to us, the manifest insufficiency of most of them and the more or less reticent or undecided character of many of those that are not simply beside the point, confirm us in our feeling that in regard to this topic there might be room for a survey of contemporary thought. We considered even the uneasiness provoked by a sustained and quite careful reading of the responses obtained, where, however, there stand out numerous valuable testimonies shot through with brief streaks of light, to reveal an unrest of much broader meaning than most of our respondents gave it. This unrest quite probably bears witness to the paroxysmal disturbance current in logical thought when it has to explain the fact that the order, the goals, and so on of nature do not coincide objectively with what they are in the mind of man, although it happens that natural necessity may agree sometimes with human necessity in such an extraordinary and exciting way that the two determinations are indiscernable. Chance having been defined as "the encounter of an external causality and an internal finality," we have to ascertain whether a certain kind of "encounter"—in this case the essential one, that is, by definition the most subjectivized one of all—can be considered under the angle of chance without our immediately seeming to beg the question. This was the most appealing of the traps we set in our questionnaire. The least we can say is that most people fell into it.

But we weren't intending to be malicious in seeking from *each* of those we approached an extremely affable answer because of our sudden and unmotivated appeal to that memory dearest to their hearts. We knew we were gratifying a desperate need to confide and to hold back, the answer to which could not help but lead the person questioned, whether in good or bad humor, to a brief philosophical discussion. Our first question was aimed mainly at involving, on the emotional level, a certain number of minds. Our second question was intended to lead them abruptly to total objectivity and to the greatest disinterest: whence the marked brevity of the two questions. You might say we had tried through this kind of formulation to extend to the mental realm the procedure of the cold shower. The reaction we expected from it met with no disappointment; in fact one of the questions managed, in a certain number of cases, to exclude the other, feeling taking over from objective rigor or giving way to it, with such and such an abstention already characteristic. In any case, the problem we were raising, arousing it from its abstraction in books, took on a passionate cast.

Making due allowance for one of the difficulties present in any inquiry, which is that since only professional writers and a few artists participate in it, the statistical interest is dubious for such a subject as ours, we have to recognize that the methodological principle of our intervention implied certain risks. In particular, the fear we had of paralyzing many of our interlocutors had we tried to decide with them on a certain precise meaning we had accepted for the words "preordained" and "fortuitous" (which would have forced us to justify and so to defend our own conception) necessarily entailed a certain ambiguity. Perhaps we underestimated this ambiguity nonetheless, because a few of our correspondents thought they could deduce the "preordained" character of the encounter from its being considered "essential" by the hypothesis itself. However, we never thought of this very pragmatic predeterminism: its observation is based on an exquisite truism.[1]

We had intended to situate the debate on a noticeably higher plane and at the very heart of this hesitation which comes over the mind when it tries to define "chance." From the outset we had first considered the sluggish evolution of this concept until now, starting with its definition in antiquity as "an accidental cause of exceptional or accessory effects taking on the appearance of finality" (Aristotle), through that of "an event brought about by the combination or the encounter of phenomena which belong to independent series in the order of causality" (Cournot), then that of an "event rigorously determined, but such that an extremely small difference in its causes would have produced a considerable difference in the facts" (Poincaré). This would lead up to its definition by the modern materialists, according to whom *chance is the form making manifest the exterior necessity which traces its path in the human unconscious* (boldly trying to interpret and reconcile Engels and Freud on this point). Suffice it to say that our question had little meaning except insofar as we intended to emphasize the ultra-objective side (corresponding to an admission of the reality of the exterior world) which the definition of chance seems to take historically.

We intended to find out if one encounter, selected among all the others in the memory, and whose circumstances therefore take on afterwards in an emotional lighting a particular relief, had been — for anyone who would care to relate it — originally placed under the sign of the spontaneous, the indeterminate, the unforeseeable, or even the unlikely and, if that were the case, in what way the reduction of these givens had come about. We were counting on every observation, even absent-minded, even apparently irrational, in order to underline that such a coincidence is in no way inextricable and to emphasize the interdependence of these two causal series (natural and human), the subtle, fleeting, and disquieting links in the present state of knowledge which can throw upon the most faltering of human steps an intense light.

Now at some distance in time I can add that probably nothing more could have been expected from a public survey on such a subject. The "circumstantial-magical," which had to be felt in its full extent and brought to an objective self-consciousness, cannot by definition become manifest except through a rigorous and sustained analysis of the chain of *circumstances* which produced it. Let us not forget that it is a question of how much one can believe in a fact or combination of facts more or less miraculous in appearance. It is possible that the dimensions of such an analysis go beyond the parameters of a survey. Perhaps it was also imprudent of us to insist on the essential character of the encounter, which resulted in giving it an emotional coefficient foreign to the real problem and more or less harmful to the understanding of its facts. Throughout this book I have had the chance to examine in some detail the character such an encounter took on in my eyes. I think I was able to do it only because of my determination to adjust progressively to this light of the anomaly whose trace is found in my preceding books.[2] My most enduring ambition will have been to disengage this unknown character from the most apparently trivial facts of my life to the most meaningful. I think I have succeeded in establishing that both kinds share a common denominator situated in the human mind, and which is none other than *desire*. What I have wanted to do above all is to show the precautions and the ruses which desire, in search of its object, employs as it wavers in preconscious waters, and, once this object is discovered, the means (so far stupefying) it uses to reveal it through consciousness.

3 At the forefront of discovery, from the moment when, for the first navigators, a new land was in sight to the moment when they set foot on the shore, from the moment when a certain learned man became convinced that he had witnessed a phenomenon, hitherto unknown, to the time when he began to measure the import of his observation—all feeling of duration abolished by the intoxicating atmosphere of *chance*—a very delicate flame highlights or perfects life's meaning as nothing else can. It is to the recreation of this particular state of mind that surrealism has always aspired, disdaining in the last analysis the prey and the shadow for what is already no longer the shadow and not yet the prey: the shadow and the prey mingled into a unique flash. Behind ourselves, we must *not let the paths of desire become overgrown.* Nothing retains less of desire in art, in science, than this will to industry, booty, possession. A pox on all captivity, even should it be in the interest of the universal good, even in Montezuma's gardens of precious stones! Still today I am only counting on what comes of my own openness, my eagerness to wander *in search* of everything, which, I am confident, keeps me in mysterious communication with other open beings, as if we were suddenly called to assemble. I would like my life to leave after it no other murmur than that of a watchman's song, of a song to while away the waiting. Independent of what happens and what does not happen, the wait itself is magnificent.[1]

I had been talking about this a few days before with Alberto Giacometti when a lovely spring day in 1934 invited us to stroll near the Flea Market, described in *Nadja* (this repetition of the setting is excused by the constant and deep transformation of the place.)[2] At this time Giacometti was working on the construction of the female figure whose photograph is reproduced in Figure 6, and this figure, although it had appeared very distinctly a few weeks before and had taken form in plaster in a few hours, underwent certain variations as it was sculpted. Whereas the gesture of the hands and the legs leaning against the plank had never caused the slightest hesitation, and the eyes, the right one figured by an intact wheel, the left one by a broken wheel, endured without change through the successive states of the figure, the length of the arms, on which the relation of the hands and breasts depended, and the angles of the face were in no way settled upon. I had never ceased to be interested in the progress of this statue, which, from the beginning, I had considered the very emanation of the *desire to love and to be loved* in search of its real human object, in its painful ignorance. As long as it had not been quite exposed, the fragility, the dynamism contained, the air of being both trapped and giving thanks, by which this graceful being had so moved me, led me to fear that in the life of Giacometti at that time any feminine intervention was likely to be harmful. Nothing was better founded than this fear, if you realize that such an intervention, passing though it was, led one day to a regrettable lowering of the hands, consciously justified by the concern to show the breasts and, having, to my great surprise, as a consequence the *disappearance of the invisible but present object* on which the interest of the figure centers, and that these hands are holding or holding up. With some slight modifications, they were reestablished the next day in their proper place. However, the head, although sketched out in its main lines, defined as to its general character, was almost alone in participating in the sentimental uncertainty from which I continue to think the work had sprung. Completely subject as it was to certain imprescribable

I had never ceased to
be interested in the progress of
this statue (p.26)
Photograph by Dora Maar

givens—venomous, astonished, and tender—it clearly resisted individualization, this resistance, as that also of the breasts to their final specification, presenting various plastic pretexts for its existence. Nevertheless, the face, so clear, so striking today, was sufficiently slow in evolving from the crystal of its plane for us to wonder if it would ever reveal its expression, by which alone the unity of the natural and the supernatural could be perfected, permitting the artist to go on to something else. There was lacking any reference to the real, something to lean on in the world of tangible objects. The term of comparison, even distant, which suddenly confers certainty was lacking.

The objects that, between the lassitude of some and the desire of others, go off to dream at the antique fair had been just barely distinguishable from each other in the first hour of our stroll. They flowed by, without accident, nourishing the meditation that this place arouses, like no other, concerning the precarious fate of so many little human constructions. The first one of them that really attracted us, drawing us as something we had *never seen,* was a half-mask of metal striking in its rigidity as well as in its forceful adaptation to a necessity unknown to us. The first bizarre idea we had was that of being in the presence of a highly evolved descendant of the helmet, letting itself be drawn into a flirtation with the velvet mask. We were able, in trying it on, to convince ourselves that the eyeholes, lined with horizontal strips of the same substance differently angled, permitted a perfect visibility above and below as well as straight in front. The flatness of the actual face, outside of the nose, accentuated by the lines leading away, rapid and delicate, to the temples, joined to a second compartmentalization of the sight by strips perpendicular to the preceding ones, and narrowing gradually, starting from the curve, lent to the top of this blind face the

A highly evolved descendant
of the helmet . . . (p.28)
Photograph by Man Ray.
© A.D.A.G.P., Paris
V.A.G.A., New York 1986

haughty attitude, *sure of itself,* and unshakable, which had struck us from the start. Although the remarkably definitive character of this object seemed to escape the merchant who urged us to buy it, suggesting we paint it in a bright color and use it as a lantern, Giacometti, usually very detached when it came to any thought of possessing such an object, put it down regretfully, seemed as we walked along to entertain some fear about its next destination, and finally retraced his steps to acquire it. Some few boutiques later, I made just as elective a choice with a large wooden spoon, of peasant fabrication but quite beautiful, it seemed to me, and rather daring in its form, whose handle, when it rested on its convex part, rose from a little shoe that was part of it. I carried it off immediately.

We were debating about the meaning that should attach to such finds, no matter how trivial they might appear.[3] The two objects, which we had been given with no wrapping, of whose existence we were ignorant some minutes before, and which imposed with themselves this abnormally prolonged sensorial contact, induced us to think ceaselessly of their concrete existence, offering to us certain very unexpected prolongations from their life. So it is that the mask, losing little by little what we had agreed on assigning it as a probable use—we had first thought we were dealing with a German mask for saber fencing—tended to situate itself in the personal research of Giacometti, taking a place in it analogous to the one that the face of the statue I just spoke of occupied. Considering all the detail of its structure, we decided that it was some-how *included* between the *Head* reproduced in number 5 of the journal *Minotaur,* the last work he had finished and whose mold he had promised me, and this face, which had remained in a sketchy state. It remained, we saw, to lift the last veil: the intervention of the mask seemed to be intended to help Giacometti overcome his

*From a little shoe that was
part of it* (p.30)
Photograph by Man Ray.
© A.D.A.G.P., Paris
V.A.G.A., New York 1986

indecision on this subject. *The finding of an object serves here exactly the same purpose as the dream, in the sense that it frees the individual from paralyzing affective scruples, comforts him and makes him understand that the obstacle he might have thought unsurmountable is cleared.*[4] A certain plastic contradiction, undoubtedly a reflection of a profound moral contradiction, observable in the first states of the sculpture, stemmed from the distinct manner in which the artist had treated the upper part–largely in planes, to flee, I suppose, certain depressing elements in the memory–and the lower part–very free, because surely unrecognizable–of the person. The mask, profiting from certain formal resemblances which must have caught our attention first (for example, as concerns the eye, the inevitable relation which can't be overlooked between the metallic trellis and the wheel), imposes, in the narrowest spatial limits, the fusion of these two styles. It seems to me impossible to underestimate its role, when I realize the perfect organic unity of this frail and imaginary body of a woman that we admire today.

Such a demonstration of the *catalyzing* role of the found object would seem less peremptory to me if that same day–but only after having left Giacometti–I had not been aware that the wooden spoon answered an analogous necessity, *although, since I am involved, this necessity remained hidden for longer*. I observe in passing that these two discoveries that Giacometti and I made *together* respond not just to some desire on the part of one of us, but rather to a desire of one of us with which the other, because of particular circumstances, is associated. I claim that this more or less conscious desire–in the preceding case the impatience to see the statue in entirety, as it should be seen–only causes a discovery by two, or more, when it is *based on typical shared preoccupations*. I would be tempted to say that the two people walking near each other constitute a single influencing body, *primed*. The found object seems to me suddenly to balance two levels of very different reflection, like those sudden atmospheric condensations which make conductors out of regions that were not before, producing flashes of lightning.

Some months earlier, inspired by a fragment of a *waking sentence,* "the Cinderella ash-tray"[5] and the temptation I had had for a long time to put into circulation some oneiric and para-oneiric objects, I had asked Giacometti to sculpt for me, according to his own caprice, a little slipper which was to be in principle Cinderella's lost slipper. I wanted to cast it in glass—even, if I remember rightly, gray glass—and then use it as an ash-tray. In spite of my frequent reminders to him of his promise, Giacometti forgot to do it for me. The *lack* of this slipper, which I really felt, caused me to have a rather long daydream, of which I think there was already a trace in my childhood. I was impatient at not being able to concretely imagine this object, over whose substance there hangs, on top of everything else, the phonic ambiguity of the word "glassy."[6] On the day of our walk, we had not spoken of this for some time.

It was when I got home and placed the spoon on a piece of furniture that I suddenly saw it charged with all the associative and interpretative qualities which had remained inactive while I was holding it. It was clearly changing right under my eyes. From the side, at a certain height, the little wood spoon coming out of its handle, took on, with the help of the curvature of the handle, the aspect of a heel and the whole object presented the silhouette of a slipper on tiptoe like those of dancers. Cinderella was certainly returning from the ball! The actual length of the spoon a minute ago had nothing definite about it, had nothing to contradict this, stretching towards the infinite as much in great size as in small: in fact the little slipper-heel presided over the spell cast, containing in itself the very *source* of the *stereotype* (the heel of this shoe heel could have been a shoe, whose heel itself. . . and so on). The wood, which had seemed intractable, took on the transparency of glass. From then on the slipper, with the shoe heel multiplying, started to look vaguely as if it were moving about alone. *This motion coincided with that of the pumpkin-carriage of the tale.* Still later the wooden spoon was illuminated as such: it took on the ardent value of one of those kitchen implements that Cinderella must have used before her metamorphosis. Thus one of the most touching teachings of the old story found itself concretely realized: the marvelous slipper potential in the modest spoon. With this idea the cycle of ambivalences found an ideal closure. Then it became clear that the object I had so much wanted to contemplate before, had been constructed outside of me, very different, *very far beyond* what I could have imagined, and regardless of many immediately deceptive elements. So it was at this price, and only at this price, that the perfect organic unity had been reached.

The sympathy existing between two or several beings seems to lead them toward solutions they would have never found on their own. This sympathy inscribes in the realm of favorable happenstance (or antipathy for unfavorable happenstance) encounters which when they take place for one being alone are not taken account of, are considered only as accidental. It would put in play, for our benefit, a veritable *second finality,* in the sense of the possible reaching of some goal by the linking of our will – on which it cannot uniquely depend – with another human will which limits itself to favoring that which we would attain. (This doubtless explains the deep reason for the surrealists' love of the game of definitions, suppositions, foresight – "What. . . If. . . When. . ."[7] – which has always seemed to me the most fabulous source of images otherwise *unfindable*). For individuals as for societies, friendship and love, the relations created by the community of suffering and the convergence of demands, are alone capable of favoring this sudden dazzling combination of phenomena which belong to independent causal series. Our fortune is scattered in the world, perhaps, and able to spread out over everything, but it is wrinkled like the bud of a poppy. When we are alone in seeking it, it closes the gate of the universe upon us, deceives us with the pitiful resemblance of all the leaves, and takes on, along the highways, the garb of so many pebbles.

1st P.S. (1934). Just as I was finishing this essay, I felt a sudden desire to follow it, in the journal that was to print it, with a new series of these Questions and Answers: "What is. . . ? – It is. . ."[8] (the answers to be supplied in complete ignorance of the questions), which bore witness to the fact that my friends and I are not inclined to become jaded, particularly not about this original system of definitions. Truthfully, it seems to me of less importance to know if certain of the answers given are able to be interchanged: I have no objection to admitting that they are, and therefore I think any calculation of probabilities useless. Similarly, it might be that instead of the spoon and the mask, other objects we could have discovered the same day would have been capable of filling the same role. – I spent a few moments picking out from the documents in my possession, the sentences which seemed to group themselves under the title "Dialogue in 1934." Since I could not literally remember them all, I was obliged, obviously, to prefer some to others. Despite my efforts at objectivity, I cannot claim to have extracted the best ones, nor the most meaningful. A conversation with Giacometti that very evening led me to think that the things omitted had not been so for very valid reasons. Returning with him to one of the reflections inspired by our stroll—that is, my incapacity, because of keeping up my *repression,* to justify fully why I needed that spoon at that moment—I remember *suddenly* that one of the definitions I had put aside (as too complicated, too easily picturesque, or so I thought) enumerated some elements which seemed disparate at first sight: spoons—and even "big" spoons—"enormous" bitter-apples, and something I couldn't recall. Just those known elements were enough to make me think that I was in the presence of a symbolic figuration of the male sexual apparatus, in which the spoon took the place of the penis. But going back to the manuscript, in order to fill in the remaining gap, removed any doubt I still had about this: "What is automatism?" someone had asked me. "Big spoons, enormous bitter-apples, chandeliers of soap bubbles." (You can see that through the delirious idea of greatness, sperm was what had tried to escape my notice the longest.) So it became clear, in these conditions, that the whole movement of my thought before this had had as its starting point the objective equation: slipper=spoon=penis=the perfect mold of this penis. Several other elements of the enigma were becoming clear: the choice of gray glass as the material in which the slipper could be conceived was explained by the desire to reconcile the two very distinct substances, "le verre," the glass (proposed by Perrault), and "le vair," ermine, its homophone,[9] whose substitution for the first word takes account of a meaningful correction (by which the fragile nature of glass is remedied and a supplementary ambiguity is created, favorable to the thesis I am advancing here. It should be noticed, moreover, that ermine fur, when it was only made up of the backs of squirrel fur, took the name *grayback,* which never fails to remind us that, for her elder sister, Perrault's heroine was called *Cucendron*).

I cannot too strongly emphasize the fact that Cinderella's slipper is just what, in our folklore, takes on the meaning of the *lost object,* so that taking myself back to the moment when I conceived the wish for its artistic realization and its possession, I can easily understand that it symbolized for me a woman *unique and unknown,* magnified and dramatized by my loneliness and by my imperious need to abolish certain memories. The need to love, with all it implies of an overwhelming need concerning its object's integrity (the case-limit of unity), finds nothing better to do here than to reproduce the actions of the prince in the fairy tale, making all the women in the kingdom try on the "most beautiful slipper in the world." The latent sexual content is transparent in the words: "Let me see," said Cinderella laughing, "if it doesn't fit me". . . "He saw that she put it on with no effort and that it fit like wax."

2nd P.S. (1936). "Of Eros and the struggle against Eros!" In its enigmatic form, this exclamation by Freud[10] happens to obsess me on certain days as only some poetry can. Rereading, two years afterwards, the preceding, I have to admit that if I succeeded in providing myself with a valid interpretation of the found spoon right away, it might have been, on the contrary, that I was quite reticent about the meaning of the mask: (1) It should be noticed that in spite of its singularity, *I don't long to possess it* but that I find a certain pleasure in Giacometti's appropriating it and that I hasten to justify this acquisition on his part. (2) After the publication in June 1934 of the preceding pages under the title "Equation of the Found Object" in the Belgian journal *Documents,* I had a long and very troubling letter from Joe Bousquet, recognizing this mask for one of those he had to hand out to his company in Argonne on a muddy evening in the war, just before the attack in which a great number of his men were to die and he was himself to get the bullet in his spine which immobilized him. I regret not being able to quote some parts of this letter, which unfortunately, and doubtless *symptomatically,* I have lost. But I remember that it insisted, in the most tragic way possible, on the evil role of this mask, not only illusory in its protection, but even awkward, heavy, distracting, *coming from another epoch,* and which had to be abandoned after this experience. (3) I recently learned that while Giacometti and I were examining this object, we had been *seen without seeing them* by two people who had just, a few seconds before, been handling the mask: one of these people, whom I lost sight of years ago, is none other than the one to whom the last pages of *Nadja* are addressed, and who is designated by the letter *X* in *Les Vases communicants,* the other being her friend. Although she was intrigued by the mask, she had put it down as I had. "Of Eros and the struggle against Eros!" My disquiet, and perhaps hers before mine, in front of the mask—about whose use I later had such painful information—the strange figure (in the form of an *X* half-dark, half-bright) formed by this encounter I was unaware of but she was not, an encounter so precisely based upon such an object, led me to think that in this moment it becomes the precipitate of the "death instinct" dominating me for so long because of the loss of a beloved being, as opposed to the sexual instinct, which, a few steps farther on, was going to be satisfied in the discovery of the spoon. There could be no more concrete a verification of Freud's statement: "The two instincts, the sexual instinct and the death instinct, behave like preservation instincts, in the strictest sense of the word, because they tend, both of them, to reestablish a state which was troubled by the apparition of life." But I had to start loving again, not just to keep on living! The two instincts, in that very way, have never been more exalted than the way they can be seen under the ultramaterial disguise of Figures 7 and 8, a disguise letting them try me out, measure their strength on me, blow by blow.

4 I confess I am hesitant to take this leap, fearing a fall into some endless unknown. Shadows of all sorts swirl rapidly about me, creating high walls whose lack of substance I am powerless to prove. Yet these same shadows seem to yield not the slightest hint about one episode of my life, so oddly moving as it was revealed to be: several times[1] I have recounted a series of facts relating to some intimate circumstances of my life, strange enough to deserve attention. Only a precise and absolutely careful reference to the emotional state of the subject to whom such things happen can furnish any basis for their evaluation. Surrealism has always suggested they be written like a medical report, with no incident omitted, no name altered, lest the arbitrary make its appearance. The revelation of the immediate, bewildering irrationality of certain events requires the most severe authentication of the human document conveying them. The time in which such a poignant interrogation is inscribed seems far too valuable to permit additions or subtractions. It can only be rendered properly by considering, and having it agreed, that it has really gone by.

But the distinction between what is plausible and what is not is no less telling for me than for others. I am no less subject than they to the need to observe how life outside me develops apart from my own individuality; if I accept to reflect at each moment as only I can upon the spectacle playing itself out beyond me, it is nevertheless odd, strangely so, to see how this spectacle suddenly appears to be set up for me alone, conforming in every way to my *previous* image of it. All the harder since that image appeared to me fantastic, and since its plainly capricious evolution rendered it unlikely in the real world: let alone a continuous corroboration, implying between events imagined and real a consistent parallelism. However rare and perhaps aleatory as it may appear, such a conjunction of circumstances is so disquieting that there can be no question of overlooking it: once established, as we have to admit, it can hold at bay all rational thinking, at least for the moment. Moreover, to be worthy of neglect, it would have to upset gravely the mind that becomes aware of it. It is in fact impossible for this mind not to experience in it both a remarkable happiness and disturbance, a mixture of *panic-provoking* terror and joy. It is as if suddenly, the deepest night of human existence were to be penetrated, natural and logical necessity coinciding, all things being rendered totally transparent, linked by a chain of glass without one link missing. If that is simply an illusion, I am ready to abandon it, but then it must be *proved* an illusion. Otherwise, if, as I believe, it may be the beginning of a contact, unimaginably dazzling, between man and the world of things, I believe we should try to see the major characteristic of that contact and try to bring about the greatest possible number of such communications, like the one I am about to describe. Only when they are observed and considered together shall we be able to determine the law according to which these mysterious exchanges between the material and mental worlds are produced. For the moment I can only call attention to them, seeing them as less exceptional than others tend to see them these days, given the suspicion about the plainly *revelatory* nature which first marks them. Speaking of revelation in our time is setting oneself up to be accused of "regressive tendencies"; I want to make it clear that I am not taking the word in its metaphysical sense, but find it the only word strong enough to render the unequalled emotion that I have had the good fortune to experience like this. The greatest weakness in contemporary thought seems to me to reside in the extravagant reverence for what we know compared with what we do not yet know. In order to show how it is obeying in this way its fundamental hatred of effort, it is more useful than usual to cite the testimony of Hegel: "The spirit is kept wakeful and lively only by its need to develop in relation to objects insofar as there remains in them something mysterious to be revealed."[2] We can surmise from this that we should not denounce, under any pretext, what may seem completely odd, if it is reliably verified.

This young woman who just entered appeared to be swathed in mist—clothed in fire? Everything seemed colorless and frozen next to this complexion imagined in perfect concord between rust and green: ancient Egypt, a tiny, unforgettable fern climbing the inside wall of an ancient well, the deepest, most somber, and most extensive of all those that I have ever leaned over, in the ruins of Villeneuve-les-Avignon, a splendid fourteenth-century French town today abandoned to gypsies. This color, taking on a deeper hue from her face to her hands, played on a fascinating tonal relation between the extraordinary pale sun of her hair like a bouquet of honeysuckle—her head bent, then raised, unoccupied—and the notepaper she asked for to write on in relation to the color of the dress, most moving perhaps now when I no longer remember it. She was very young, but her distinctive youth did not strike me at first sight, because of this illusion she gave of moving about, in broad daylight, within the gleam of a lamp. I had already seen her here two or three times, her coming announced before I saw her each time by an undefinable quiver moving from one pair of shoulders to the next, from the door of this café toward me. For me this motion itself, which, as it is disturbing to a common assembly, quickly assumes a hostile character, has always, whether in art or in life, signalled the presence of the *beautiful*. And I can certainly say that here, on the twenty-ninth of May 1934, this woman was *scandalously* beautiful. Such a certainty, in itself exciting enough for me at that epoch, was likely, moreover, to obsess me entirely during the time that elapsed between her real appearances, because from the first moments, a quite vague intuition had encouraged me to imagine that the fate of that young woman could some day, no matter how tentatively, be entwined with mine. I had just some days earlier written the beginning text of this present book, a text which takes full account of the mental and emotional dispositions at that time: a need to reconcile the idea of unique love with its more or less sure denial in the present social framework, the need to prove that a solution, more than sufficient, indeed in excess of the vital problems, can always be expected when one deserts ordinary logical attitudes. I have never ceased to believe that, among all the states through which humans can pass, love is the greatest supplier of solutions of that kind, being at the same time in itself the ideal place for the joining and fusion of these solutions. People despair of love stupidly – I have despaired of it myself – they live in servitude to this idea that love is always behind them, never *before* them: bygone years, lies about forgetting after twenty years. They can bear to admit – and force themselves to – that love is not *for them,* with its procession of clarities, with this look it casts upon the world from all the eyes of diviners. They are limping with fallacious memories, for which they even invent the origin of an immemorial fall, so as not to find themselves too guilty. And yet for each, the promise of each coming hour contains life's whole secret, perhaps about to be revealed one day, possibly in another being.

This young woman who had just entered was writing – she had also been writing the evening before, and I had already agreeably supposed very quickly that she might have been writing to *me,* and found myself awaiting her letter. *Naturally,* nothing. At seven-thirty, on May 29, she once again assumed the same attitude – looking at the ceiling, the pen, a wall, the ceiling, her gaze never meeting mine – making me slightly impatient. If I moved a bit, her eyes, raised for a long time, did not blink, or hardly at all: they cast, at a distance from me, their long absent fire of dry grasses, and her graceful torso took possession again of the stillness. I gradually felt myself disturbed by a question that made silence difficult. How near that moment seems! I know so little of what was impelling me. But this room, fully lit, was free of any other presence; a last wave had swept away my friends to whom I was still talking.

This young woman who had just entered was just about to reappear in the street, where I was waiting for her without being seen. In the street. . . The marvelous rush of evening made this liveliest and, at times, most disquieting part of Montmartre glitter like no other. And this figure was fleeing before me, ceaselessly intercepted by the darkness of moving hedges. Hope—what sort of hope?—was now just a tiny flame flickering beside me. And the sidewalks forked off inexplicably one after the other, in an itinerary just as capricious as possible. Despite appearances to the contrary, I wondered if I hadn't been noticed, so that I was being led deliberately into the most marvelous roundabout path.[3] All the same, it led some-where, to some parking place. One more step, one less step, and, astonished, the face I had feared in a frenzy never to see again was there, and so close, turned towards me, that its smile in that moment leaves me even today with the memory of a squirrel hold-ing a green hazelnut. Hair in a bright downpour upon flowering chestnut trees. . . She tells me she has written me—this letter just now was destined for me—and was surprised no one had given it to me, and, as I was totally unable of thinking then how to retain her, she rapidly said farewell to me, giving me a rendezvous for that same evening at midnight.

I shall glide over the tumultuous hours that ensued. It is two in the morning when we leave the Café of the Birds. My self-confidence undergoes a peculiar crisis, sufficiently grave for me to think it necessary to give some idea of it here if I still want to clarify the immediate results of this encounter insofar as they are apparently almost normal and, upon reflection, on another level so rigorously in harmony as to be absolutely inexplicable. To the extent that I was able to dwell for a few days on the idea so *a priori* purely seductive that I can be in some sense awaited, even sought, by a being to whom I ascribe such charm, the fact that this idea has just been given some real basis can only precipitate me into an abyss of negations. What am I capable of after all, and what shall I do so as not to be unworthy of such a fate? I walk ahead automatically, in a great clank of gates being closed. To love, to find once more the lost grace of the first moment when one is in love. . . All sorts of defenses take shape around me, bright laughter springing up from the years past to finish sobbing, under the great beating of gray wings of an uncertain spring night. Uncertain: this uncertainty is in me, since, on that night, I find myself reading into the future what could be, what should be if the heart were to *rule*. Freedom in relation to other beings, freedom in relation to the person one has been seems only to show itself so tempting in order to weigh me down with its challenge. Who goes with me in this hour in Paris without leading me and whom, moreover, I am not leading? I never remember having felt in my life such a great weakness. I almost lose sight of myself, I seem to have been carried away in my turn like the actors in the first scene. The conversation which, as long as my too lovely interlocutor remained seated across from me, slipped effortlessly from one subject to the next, now grazes only the mask of things. I fear I am letting it slip into the artificial in spite of myself. I am reduced to stopping from time to time to hold immobile before me the face that I can no longer stand to see only in profile, but this childish behavior reassures me very briefly. Perhaps it would soon become suddenly impossible to take a step, without the help of an arm which has just taken my own, recalling me to real life while enlightening me with its pressure about the shape of a breast.

While we are lingering an hour later in the tiny streets of Les Halles, I regret all the more sharply the eclipse of that breast when it becomes too hard to walk side by side among the trucks in this increasing noise, which mounts like the sea towards the immense appetite of the next day. My gaze and some magnificent white, red, and green cubes of the first vegetables of the season slide unfortunately upon the sidewalk, gleaming with horrendous garbage. It is also the hour when bands of revelers begin to pour out in this region to finish the night in some celebrated greasy spoon, sounding in the vigorous rhythms of honest work the black, equivocal, and gauzy note of evening clothes, furs, and silks. Come now, it is only in fairy tales that doubt cannot sneak in, that it is never a question of slipping on some fruit peeling. I see bad and good in all their native state, the bad winning out with all the ease of suffering: the idea that it is perhaps the only way, in the long run, to create the good perhaps no longer even grazes my mind. Life is slow, and man scarcely knows how to play it. The possibilities of finding the one being who could help him to play it, to give it its full sense, are lost in the chart of stars. Who is going with me, who is preceding me tonight once again? Tomorrow is still made up of determining factors to be accepted whether one wills or not, without taking any account of these charming curls, or of these no less charming ankles. There would still be time to turn back.

If I am speaking only the language I have been taught, what will ever serve as a signal that we should listen to the voice of unreason,

The tiny streets of Les Halles (p.45)
Photograph by Brassaï.
© Gilberte Brassaï 1986

claiming that tomorrow will be *other*, that it is entirely and mysteriously separated from yesterday? I was near you again, my beautiful wanderer, and you showed me, in passing, the Tour Saint-Jacques under its pale scaffolding, rendering it for some time now the world's great monument to the hidden. You know how I loved that tower: yet I see now again a whole violent existence forming around it to include us, to contain wildness itself in its gallop of clouds about us:

> In Paris the Tour Saint-Jacques swaying
> Like a sunflower,[4]

I said, I thought rather obscurely, in a poem, and I have understood since then that this wavering of the tower was above all my own hesitation between the two French meanings of the word *tournesol*, designating at the same time this kind of helianthus, also known as the great sun, and the reactive agent used in chemistry, usually as a blue litmus paper reddening at the contact of an acid. Still, the meeting of the two meanings in this fashion portrays correctly the complex conception I form of the tower, of its somber magnificence, like that of the flower rising like it, quite alone upon a more or less impoverished corner of the earth, and of the rather troubling circumstances which presided over its construction, to which, clearly, the age-old dream of the transmutation of metals is closely linked. Even the change from blue to red as the specific property of the reactive-sunflower can be justified by analogy with the distinctive colors of Paris whose cradle this quarter of the city is, of Paris shown here in a quite specially organic and *essential* way by its Hotel de Ville, on our left as we walk towards the Latin Quarter. I succumb to the wonderful dizziness these places inspire in me, places where everything I have best known began. I have, suddenly, disposed of the previous reductive representations which had been threatening me just now; I am free from everything that could persuade me that it is impossible to distinguish my affective

In Paris the Tour Saint-Jacques swaying . . . (p.47)
Photograph by Brassaï. © Gilberte Brassaï 1986

self from yesterday's character. Let this curtain of shadows be lifted and let me be led fearlessly toward the light! Turn, oh sun,[5] and you, oh great night, banish from my heart everything that is not faith in my new star!

The brisk wind carrying us along may never die down: it is from now on perfumed, as if tiers of gardens were to be raised above us. We have reached the Quai aux Fleurs just as the mass of rose-colored earthenware pots arrive, on whose base all tomorrow's active seduction is predicated and concentrated. The morning passersby soon about to haunt this market will miss much of the emotion that can emanate from the spectacle of the floral arrangements when they are really in contact with the city pavement. It is marvelous to see them for the last time assembled by types atop the wagons bringing them in, as if they had been born like unto each other from their very conception, still numb from the night and still so free of any contact that they seem to have been transported in immense dormitories. Motionless upon the earth before me, they fall asleep once more, huddled against each other in pairs as far as the eye can see. Soon it will be June, and the heliotrope will be bending its thousands of crests over to look in the round black mirrors of the wet earth. Elsewhere, the begonias recompose in patience their great rose window with its dominant solar red, causing even the window of Notre Dame over there to go pale. All the flowers, even the least exuberant in this climate, delight in mingling their strength as if to restore to me the youth of feeling. A clear fountain where my desire to take a new being along with me is reflected and comes to slake its thirst, the desire for that which has not yet been possible – to go together down the path lost with the loss of childhood, winding along, perfuming the woman still unmet, the woman to come amid the prairies. Are you, at last,

This kind of helianthus (p.47
Photograph by Man Ray.
© A.D.A.G.P., Paris
V.A.G.A., New York 1986

this woman? is it only today you were to come? While, as if in dream, with still other flowerbeds before us, you lean long over these flowers enveloped in shadow as if less to breathe in their perfume than to snatch their secret from them, and such a gesture, by itself alone, is the most moving response you could make to this question which I am not asking you. This profusion of wealth at our feet can only be interpreted as a luxurious advance made by life toward me, and more obviously still, through you. And moreover, you are so blond, so attractive in the morning dawn, that it understates the case to say that you cannot be separated from this radiant expansion.

.   .   .   .

From this point everything starts afresh; from this point there radiate—we must keep silent—too many reasons to mingle into the tale all the tenses of the verb *to be*. I shall probably consent to that one day when it is time to establish, as I put it to myself, that true love is, while it lasts, subject in no way to any noticeable change. Only a more or less resigned adaptation to present social conditions will make us admit that the phantasmagoria of love is uniquely produced by our knowing the beloved being so little: I mean it is supposed to cease at the instant when this being is no more concealed. This belief in the mind's sudden abandon, in such a case, of all its most exalting and rarest faculties, can naturally only be explained by a usually atavistic relic of a religious education, ready to see that humans will always be willing to put off the possession of truth and happiness, to defer any wish for the integral accomplishment of desire to a fictitious "beyond," which on further scrutiny turns out to be, moreover—as it has been so well said—only another "on this side." However much, as I have so often said, I wanted to react against this way of looking, it is not up to me to dispense with it all alone, and I shall limit myself today, in passing, to deploring

the continual sacrifices in its honor which, for many centuries, poets have felt themselves obliged to make. It is the whole modern conception of love which should be reexamined, such as is commonly but transparently expressed in phrases like "love at first sight" and "honeymoon." All this shoddy terminology is, on top of that, tainted with the most reactionary irony: but I do not intend to question it further now. It is in fact from the thought of what happened to me *this first day* and of my subsequent return on this occasion to certain already ancient premises (moreover quite inexplicable) underlying the facts in question that I want a new light to come. It is only by making evident the intimate relation linking the two terms *real* and *imaginary* that I hope to break down the distinction, which seems to me less and less well founded, between the subjective and the objective.[6] Only the contemplation of this relationship leads me to wonder if the idea of *causality* doesn't turn out to have run quite dry. Only by underlining the continuous and perfect coincidence of two series of facts considered—until further notice—as rigorously independent, do I intend to justify and advocate more and more choice of a *lyric behavior* such as it is indispensable to everyone, even if for only an hour of love, such as surrealism has tried to systematize it, with all possible predictive force.

One of the first mornings following this long night walk in Paris, I was getting dressed without consciously thinking of these last events. At such moments, I do not usually worry about questions of any importance to me. In general my mind remains distracted, to the extent that some song lyric or other might drift through it—I have very little musical memory—lyrics to which I sometimes vocalize with some timidity, especially if they are accompanied by very old melodies or by the ten o'clock sun of Offenbach's operettas.

At other times, there drift through some poems recomposing themselves more or less slowly, the most remarkable thing about them being that they occur in my memory almost always preceded by the intonation that I might give if reading them aloud, traces from that remaining in the visual reading. I have often been amazed, on that topic, at having such a precise idea of their value even before they have begun to organize themselves, feeling for their author, about whom I have no clue yet, a characteristic sympathy or antipathy just from this murmur, a feeling that never fails to justify itself afterwards. That particular morning it was not quite the same, since the poem was mine—I recognized it without enthusiasm: there were some rather short fragments, some vague bits of a poem which had formerly appeared under my signature and which tried to fit themselves together without doing so. I could scarcely distinguish today which of them came nearest to being recollected in detail, in the way that some animals—dogs, owls, monkeys—proffer some sounds which seem to have some meaning in the air which is also our air, but our ears are turned to the wrong side, or then I just don't understand. This poem was special in that I did not like it and never had, to the point that I had avoided publishing it in two successive collections: a book where I tried to collect what I then thought were my best poems with some others, on one hand; and *A Little Poetic Anthology of Surrealism* on the other. And yet the "poems" I had written were so few that I did not have much choice. It was, to be specific, an *automatic* poem: written on the spot or so nearly that it could pass for such in 1923, when I included it in *Earth Light.*[7] However criticized and even obscurely rejected it was afterwards, I scarcely see how to speak of the involuntary, fragmentary quotations that I was making from it all of a sudden, except in the same way as those sentences of the half-waking state of which I said in 1924 in the *Surrealist Manifesto* that they were "tapping on the window." Those quotations, I must admit, were still tapping on that window, but quite weakly, and I had, on that same afternoon, to go out and wander around alone before I noticed that a remarkable need for cohesion had taken hold of them, that they would not let me go until they had been returned to the entity, organic or not, to which they belonged. So I was led, only in the evening, to reopen one of my books at the page where I knew I would pick them out. This concession to everything I hadn't wanted to know until then turned out to be a brilliant and uninterrupted suite of discoveries:

SUNFLOWER

for Pierre Reverdy

The traveler passing through the Halles at summerfall
Was walking on her tiptoes
Despair was swirling its great lovely calla lilies in the sky
And in the handbag was my dream that flask of salts
Only God's godmother had breathed
Torpor spread like mist
At the Smoking Dog Café
Where the pro and the con had just come in
The young woman could scarcely be seen by them,
   and only askance
Was I speaking with the ambassadress of saltpeter
Or of the white curve on black ground we call thought
The Innocents' Ball was in full swing
Chinese lanterns caught fire slowly among the chestnut trees
The lady with no shadow knelt on the Pont-au-Change
Rue Gît-le-Coeur the stamps were no longer the same
Nighttime pledges were kept at last
Homing pigeons helping kisses

Met with the breasts of the lovely stranger
Pointing through the crepe of perfect meanings
A farm prospered in the heart of Paris
And its windows looked out on the Milky Way
But no one lived there yet because of the chance comers
Comers more devoted still, we know, than ghosts[8]
Some of them seem to swim like that woman
And in love there enters a bit of their substance
She interiorizes them
I am the pawn of no sensual power
And yet the cricket singing in the ashen hair
One evening near the statue of Etienne Marcel
Gave me a knowing look
André Breton it said go on[9]

Trying to place this poem exactly in time, I think I can establish that it was written in May or June 1923, in Paris. I would desperately have liked to find the manuscript, perhaps with a date on it, but the latter must remain in the possession of a person from whom it would be too embarrassing to borrow it. In particular, it would be extremely valuable for me to know if it has anything crossed out, for I still now have that hesitation in my mind which I must have had when I put certain words in it. Two or three changes have no doubt been made in it since the original version, with the intention—so regrettable in the long run—of rendering it more homogeneous, reducing the immediate, apparently arbitrary obscurity that I was led to find in it the first time I read it. This poem always presented itself to me as *really inspired* in the connected action it contains, but this inspiration, except in the last third of "Sunflower," never seemed to me expressed without some letdown in the actual *trouvaille* of words. From the point of view of style, such a text offers to my eyes and ears certain weaknesses and gaps. What can I say of my subsequent attempt to remedy that? Today I am unhesitatingly convinced of its profound failure. The critical activity, which suggested to me *a posteriori* certain substitutions or additions of words, now enables me to see these corrections as faults: they do not help the reader–rather the contrary–and only manage here and there to prejudice the authenticity. I shall take as examples *a few* of these slight alterations (they have been so unsatisfactory for me that they remain ineffaceable spots after thirteen years): the introduction of the prepositional phrase *d'eux* (by them) between *vue* (seen) and *que mal* (only askance) in the ninth line, the replacement of the *à* by *de* at the beginning of the eleventh. Nor can I hide the fact that the word *dévoués* (devoted) stands, in the twenty-third line, in the place of another, perhaps the word *dangereux* (dangerous)–in any case some word the pen refused to trace under the pretext that it would have produced a puerile impression alongside the word *revenants* (ghosts); *dévoués,* in any case, is here empty of any content, a wig of an epithet. I should just have left three dots here. . .

With these slight reservations, I believe it is possible to confront the purely imaginary adventure which is framed in the poem and the later realization–impressive in its rigor–of this adventure in life itself. It goes without saying, in fact, that in writing the poem "Sunflower" I was helped by no prior representation which might have explained to me the peculiar direction I was taking. Not only did "la voyageuse," "la jeune femme," "la dame sans ombre"–the traveler, the young woman, the lady with no shadow–remain for me a faceless creature, but in relation to the circumstantial unwinding of the poem I had nothing according to which I could orient myself. Necessarily, the final mysterious injunction only seemed all the more important to me and doubtless because of it, and also the detailed character of this tale of something *which nevertheless didn't happen,* the poem, which I had considered for a long time very unsatisfactory, was not immediately destroyed like so many others.

The traveler walking on tiptoe: It would be impossible not to recognize in her the now very silent passerby of May 29, 1934. The "summerfall": the fall of the day and the fall of the night are, as everyone knows, synonymous. The arrival of night is therefore, certainly, included in this image, where it is combined with summer's arrival.

Despair: At this moment, in fact, immense, as great as the hope which has just been aroused, sinking so suddenly and which will be reborn. I feel myself losing some of my assurance in the presence of the sexual meaning of the calla lily and of the handbag, which, although it tries to hide behind delirious ideas of grandeur – the stars, "God's godmother" (?) – is no less clear. The "flask of salts" in question here is moreover, at present, the only element of the poem which has eluded my patience, my interpretative constancy. I still remain hostile to the fourth and fifth lines, almost entirely responsible for the disfavor in which I have held this "Sunflower." I have nevertheless, as we will see later, all too many reasons for admitting that what becomes apparent most slowly from the analysis is what is simplest and what must be accorded greatest value, not to think that here is an essential element, which will become transparent to me some day.

The Smoking Dog (Le Chien qui fume): This was for me the typical name of one of these restaurants in Les Halles I was speaking of. The "torpor" is doubtless this time only mine: I won't hide an intense need to escape, to take refuge in sleep in order to avoid certain decisions I feared making. What had become of me until now was struggling (I think I have been sufficiently clear about this) with what I could still become. The comfort of every next day's life was already defined; my concern not to interfere with the moral existence of the irreproachable being who had spent the time preceding this by my side, joined with the novelty and the irresistible strength of the attraction I was feeling ("the pro and the con") kept me in a most painfully ambivalent state.

Could scarcely see, only askance: I have explained this evident disadvantage, a result for me, I think, of walking.

The two hypotheses about the passerby, the meaning of her intervention: That was the way I formulated them for myself: did the temptation which I felt in regard to her coincide with the still greater one toward danger? Doesn't it still sparkle, moreover, like phosphorous, with all the particular intentions my mind is hiding? (I repeat that these intentions had been given, more than ever, free rein in the text called "Beauty will be convulsive," written a few days before.)

The Innocents' Ball: We are approaching, no doubt about it, the Tour Saint-Jacques. The Ossuary of the Innocents, later made into a market and now evoked concretely only by the central fountain, with Jean Goujon's water nymphs in the square of the same name[10] – the nymphs seem to have presided over the loveliest spell of this tale – serves here to introduce Nicolas Flamel, who had the famous arcade there built at the end of the fourteenth century, with his initials (on this arcade we know he had had a black man painted, turned towards a gilt plaque on which Venus or Mercury was represented with an eclipse of the sun and of the moon; this man was holding at arm's length a scroll covered with the inscription: "A marvel I see which astonishes me greatly").

Chinese lanterns: Only weeks after meeting her did I learn that at the music hall where my companion of this first night used to appear, the director of the establishment had one day called her publicly the Fourteenth of July and that this nickname, in this place, had stuck to her. I might have been seen, approaching her, associating the light of chestnut trees with her hair.

Le Pont-au-Change: The exactness of this episode, the movement towards the flowers it depicts so well, are sufficiently striking for me not to have to dwell on them.

Rue Gît-le-Coeur: There would be no use either in commenting even in passing on the name of this street (Here-Lies-the-Heart), which makes such a violent contrast with the feeling expressed unreservedly in the following verse.

The homing pigeons: Through her cousin, with whom I had in the past been sharing some thoughts, she had, she confided, heard of me for the first time; it was he who had given her the wish to know my books, which, in their turn, had made her want to know me. Now, that young man was just doing his military service at that period, and I had received from him, a few days earlier, a letter stamped with Sfax, with the seal of a *colombophile* center where he was stationed.

Helping kisses: Assimilated as they are to the homing pigeons, they take account, in the least figurative way, of the necessity I feel of making a gesture which, however, I refuse myself, a necessity in no way strange to the rallying points in the street I have mentioned. The kisses, here, are no less situated in possibility by being placed between the homing pigeons (the idea of an agreeable person) and the breasts about which, in the course of the tale, I was led to say that they took away any courageous impulse toward renunciation.

A farm in the middle of Paris: The whole countryside irrupts at this moment in the poem, resulting naturally from what had until then only been obscurely longed for. Even the idea of agricultural culti-vation contained in the word "farm" is supported by the spectacle that the Flower Market offers fleetingly at this hour of the night.

The chance comers (as opposed to the *returners* or *ghosts*): The unrest shown in the poem as soon as this word appears (with its immediate repetition, the near lapsus I spoke of) seems to me to have as its starting point the emotion expressed, at the news of this encounter, by the woman then sharing my life, at the idea that I could be seek-ing the companionship of a new woman (whereas she was suppor-tive of my wish to see again another woman, for whom I had a great tenderness).

Seeming to swim: Quite remarkable; even after I had ascertained that on all the other points I should take "Sunflower" for a *prophetic* poem, I tried in vain to limit that odd observation, to which it was impossible to grant the slightest significative value. Let me again stress the fact that the verse which I am referring to had immediately appeared awkward. I must say that it had suffered straight off from a comparison I had made between it and a line of Baudelaire, and that, no matter how much I admired the comparison of feminine gait to the art of dance, I found the comparison with swimming much less fortunate. I don't know what could have hidden from

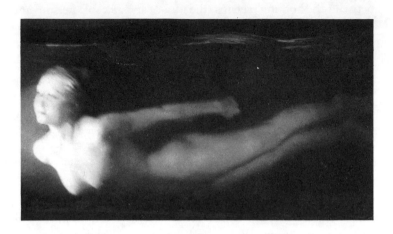

Seeming to swim . . . (p.61)
Photograph by Rogi André

me for so long the real content, completely different, the particularly direct meaning of these words: the music-hall "number" in which the young woman appeared every day was a swimming number. "Seemed to swim," insofar as it was opposed for me to "seemed to dance," said of a woman walking, may even have the meaning here of "seems to dance under the water," a description which my friends who saw her moving about in the pool would accept, as would I.

She interiorizes them: In concentrating in herself all the power of these "chance comers," without helping me to have some precise idea of the kind of interest she bears me, she is at this moment all the more perilous as she is more silent, more secret.

Of no sensual power: The extremely rapid and prosaic form of this declaration seems to me characteristic of the movements through which I passed last night. Abstracted from the projective conditions of the poem in real life long after, it would be impossible for me not to consider it gratuitous and inopportune. But, in a way apparently suited to the occasion, it marks the height of my inner agitation: I have just been speaking about love, all the sublimating forces rush to intervene, and already I am anxiously forbidding myself from succumbing to the illusions of desire.

The cricket: The first time I heard a cricket chirp in Paris was a few days after that, in the same room filled with the animating spirit of that springtime night I recounted. The window of this room, in a hotel of the Rue Faubourg-Saint-Jacques, opened onto the courtyard of the Lying-In Hospital, where the insect must have been hiding. It continued, after that, to make its presence known every evening.

I couldn't help later, in evoking this courtyard, considering as a most striking prediction of my coming there the anecdote that I tell in *Les Vases communicants* (accompanying a girl in the street, I confuse the Lariboisière Hospital with the Lying-In Hospital). Nevertheless, I had at that time no way of representing that place concretely: the magnificent cries of pain and of joy which rise from it at any hour had not yet reached my ears.[11] But this cricket especially, this cricket whose chirp was so important for me in completing the two combined itineraries of the poem and the stroll, what is it and what does it tend to symbolize in all this? I have often reflected on that, and every time, I have succeeded only in recalling that passage from Lautréamont: "Have you ever noticed the gracefulness of a pretty cricket moving about in the Paris sewers? Only this one: it was Maldoror! Magnetizing the flourishing capitals, with a pernicious fluid, he induces in them a lethargic state where they are incapable of keeping up their guard, as they should."[12] Magnetizing the flourishing capitals. . . with a pernicious fluid. . . It is all too clear, in any case, that the cricket, in the poem as in life, intervenes to take away all my doubts. The statue of Etienne Marcel, flanking one of the façades of the Hotel de Ville, doubtless designates in the poem the heart of Paris beating throughout the stroll, as we have seen, in unison with mine.

.   .   .   .

I have insisted, especially in *Les Vases communicants,* on the fact that self-analysis alone is, in many cases, capable of *exhausting* the content of dreams, and that this analysis, if it is thorough enough, leaves none of the *residue* that might permit us to attribute a transcendental character to oneiric activity. On the other hand, it seems to me that I have cut off all too quickly when I had to explain that, similarly, self-analysis could sometimes exhaust the content of real events, to the point of making them depend entirely on the least conscious prior activity of the mind. The concern I had, on the revolutionary level, for not cutting myself off from practical action, perhaps kept me from pushing my thoughts to their limits, given the difficulty of making most of the revolutionaries *of that period* share such a dialectically rigorous point of view. Not having been able to pass over to practical action, I feel today no scruples in returning to it, all the more since I think this time I have a far more conclusive document than the one I had relied on until that time.

I say that there isn't anything in this poem of 1923 that did not announce the most important thing to happen to me in 1934. Were there to be any doubt about the future necessity of the dedication of the poem, that doubt would not evaporate, as we will see. Less than two months after what I have called "the night of the sunflower" – it was precisely July 23, in the morning – I had had a long conversation with René Char and Paul Eluard about the incredible coincidences that had just come about; then I had left them to go to lunch in the restaurant.[13] The nearest restaurant was none other than the one I spoke of at the end of the first chapter of this book in connection with a wide-reaching poetic conversation I had overheard there on April 10. I had taken only a few steps to get there when I changed my mind, fearing to find myself too alone in that place which, for a long time now, the strange servant of whom I spoke no longer lit up with her highly ambiguous smile of a pretty goat. When I met my friends, I found them still talking about what we had just discussed. Char, in particular, had raised the question of this dedication, remarking that the only two poems I had dedicated to Pierre Reverdy bore, respectively, the associated titles of "Clé de sol" and "Tournesol."[14] I could at the moment propose no other rational explanation than this one: I had always liked this name, Pierre Reverdy, to which I must have unconsciously given this prolongation: stone rolling no more, stone gathering moss.[15] The idea of such a stone is visually agreeable to me, and still strengthened in me by the memory of that *Willow Street,* constructed like the bed of a stream, which I used always to climb joyfully to go to see Reverdy on certain mornings of 1916 and 1917. I must say, moreover, that very often there sings in my memory one of his lines,

A fist on reality really full

a line which I hope I am not misquoting and which most perfectly sums up the teaching that his poetry has been for me. And then there would be nothing extraordinary in the word "sol" (sun, but also ground: to touch the ground, not to lose your footing) being associated in my mind most particularly with this name, of which I am prepared to think that it has as its function reestablishing, in the case of the two poems, the equilibrium upset particularly in favor of bewilderment ("Clé de sol," or the "key of G," transposes the emotion that I felt at the announcement of the death of Jacques Vaché).[16] About two hours after picking up this conversation again, Char, who had accompanied me to the town hall of the 17th arrondissement, showed me, on the wall facing the window where I was waiting to be handed some public document, a poster unique of its kind, bearing in heavy black letters against a white background these words, which seemed so decisive then: "Reverdy's Heritage."

It only remains for me, in explaining the value of the purely spiritual presentation of this marvelous adventure, to call attention as forcefully as possible to the irrational character of the dialogue of April 10, to which I allude above, and to the need, scarcely less irrational, that I felt to reproduce it without commentary at the end of an essentially theoretical text. Let the reader go back to that remarkably alert and mysterious scene the playing out of which is ruled by these words no less imperative than those of the cricket in the poem: "Here, l'Ondine." It is as if the only naiad, the only living mermaid in this tale, quite different from the person addressed, who, moreover, was going to disappear now, had been able to do nothing but answer this call. A further proof of it is that she tried during this period to rent an apartment in the house just across from the restaurant in question here, on the avenue Rachel.

The following August 14, I married the all-powerful commander of the night of the sunflower.

5 The peak of the Teide in Tenerife is made from the sparks glancing off the little play dagger that the pretty Toledan ladies keep day and night against their breasts.

You ascend by an elevator for several hours, your heart switching unnoticed to a white-red, your eyes closing at the series of landing stages. Far below, the little lunar squares with their benches hovering around a pond whose bottom seems scarcely any shinier under the weight of a ring of water and the illusory foam of a few swans, all of that cut out from the same blue ceramic with large white flowers. There, just in the depths of the bowl around whose rim nothing is gliding to make it sing in the morning except the free flight of the canary native to the island, there it is that, while the night falls, the young girl's heel, beginning to rise with a secret, speeds up its scale. I am thinking about the girl whom Picasso painted some thirty years ago, whose innumerable copies cross at Santa Cruz from one sidewalk to another, in dark costumes, with that ardent look turning away only to regain its liveliness elsewhere like a fire running across the snow. The incandescent stone of the sexual unconscious, as unparticularized as possible, apart from any

The girl whom Picasso painted
some thirty years ago (p.67)
Photograph by Galerie Simon

idea of immediate possession, forms again at this depth as at no other, all being lost in the first modulations, which are also the last, of the unheard phoenix. We have gone past the peak of the coral trees through which its scarlet wing appears and whose thousand intertwined rose grills forbid anyone's perceiving the difference between a leaf, a flower, and a flame. They were like so many fires enamored of the houses, content to exist near them without embracing them. The fiancées were shining in the windows, lit with a single indiscreet branch, and their voices, alternating with those of the young men below, ardent for them, mingled with the perfumes unloosed in the May night in a restless murmur, vertiginous as the signal, over the silk of the deserts, of the Sphinx approaching. The question stirring so many breasts gracefully at this moment was in fact, posed as it was in the *optimal* conditions of time and place, that of the future of love – the future of one single love, and in virtue of that, of all love.

We have gone past the peak of the coral trees, and already have to turn our heads to see their rose-colored ramp swaying over this corner of the eternal fable. The arena has unfolded in its turn according to the twist of the dusty paths up which the crowd's acclamations rose the Sunday before, at this minute when man, concentrating on himself all the pride of men and the desire of women, has only to hold up on the tip of his sword the mass of bronze with a luminous crescent that really, *suddenly* is stamping, the admirable bull with the amazed eyes. Then blood, not this vitreous water we have these days, gushed cascading down to the sea. The little children on the terrace could see nothing but the blood; they had probably been brought there in the hope that they would get used to spilling it, theirs and that of some familiar monster, in the uproar and sparkle that excuse everything. Since they couldn't yet spill blood, they were spilling milk. Between the martyred blooms of the cacti, none of whose spiny clumps they left intact at a reasonable distance from the road (acting in league with the cochineals and the goats) – nothing keeps the thought of misery more alive than these plants, exposed as they are to all the affronts and disposing of such an amazing power to scar over – here a hundred-branch chandelier of a spurge with a stem as thick as your arm but three times longer, which, hit by a stone, bleeds abundantly white and stains. Little children take delighted aim at this plant from far off, and it must be admitted that the secretion exposed in this way is the most disturbing thing imaginable. Impossible not to associate with it the idea of mother's milk and also that of ejaculation. The impossible pearl gathers and rolls down inexplicably over the side of some hexagonal prism of green velvet turned towards us. Guilty feelings cannot be far off. Invulnerable in its essence, the attacked spine clump spurts forth completely new as far as the eye can reach in the stony field. It's not the one who has most suffered from the staining.

When you are cast into the spiral of the island shell so as to see only the three or four first great twistings, it seems to split in two so as to present itself in section with one half standing, the other oscillating in even beat upon the dazzling base of the sea. Here, in the brief succeeding intervals of the superb milk hydras, the last houses grouped in the sun, with their stucco façades of colors unknown in Europe, like a deck of cards with the backs marvelously dissimilar and nevertheless bathed in the same light, uniformly discolored by all the time for which the pack has been shuffled. The pack of several generations of sailors. The white ships are dreaming in the rails, Ariadnes through all their hair of stars and their armpits of climates. The immense peacock of the sea comes back to spread its tail at all the turnings. All the relative shadow, all the circle of cells buzzing with daylight smaller and smaller towards the interior of the crozier, reposes on the plantations of black banana shrubs, with flowers of factories whence there issue forth the horns of young bulls. All the shadow cast over the sea is made of the great stretches of even blacker sand which make up so many beaches like that of Puerto Cruz, interchangeable strips between the water and the land, specked with obsidian on their edge by the retreating waters. Black sand, sand of the nights running away so much more quickly than light sand, I have never been able to stop myself from trembling when being given the mysterious power of having you slide between my fingers. Just the reverse of what was for me at fifteen the limit of what I could hope for, to set out for the unknown with a woman at dusk on a white road, I sense today all the emotion of the physical goal attained by treading the unknown with the one I love, the magnificent flowerbed the color of the time when I used to imagine that the tuberose was black.

A final farewell to the black sand, no, for the more you rise, the more you will be present at the contraction of its mother stems, the great lava flows running to lose themselves in the volcano's heart. They bend at the will of the forests donned by the multi-colored variety of orchids, the forests rapidly turning to brush. At the first onset of coolness, you may stop, and, from this point where everything starts to be in such bitter lack, you may solicit, as if by enchantment, the most madly exuberant point of the island, reaching it as the crow flies.

I enjoy passing through this rough form of desire. Nothing easier than returning to the depths of the *self* as probably this sudden, too rapid impoverishment of nature invites me to do, to provide

Of even blacker sand . . . (p.71)

myself with the illusion of recreating the world at once. Nowhere other than in Tenerife would I have been able to hold nearer together the two points of the compass with which I touched simultaneously everything that can be taken away, everything that can be given. What tended to be most desperately lacking took its value above all from what grew in such profusion so nearby. I regret having discovered so late these ultrasensitive parts of the earth.

At the foot of Teide and under the watch of the greatest dracaena in the world, the Orotava Valley reflects in a pearl sky the whole treasure of vegetal life, otherwise sparse between regions. The immense tree, plunging its roots in prehistory, hurls into the day as yet unsoiled by the apparition of man its irreproachable mast, which suddenly bursts apart in oblique masts, radiating out in a completely regular rhythm. It shoulders with all its strength intact these still living shadows among us which are those of the kings of the Jurassic fauna whose traces you find once more as soon as you scrutinize the human libido. I like its being the dracaena, in its perfect immobility, the dracaena plant only apparently asleep, standing on the threshold of the palace of foliage of the garden of four seasons of the Orotava ready to defend the eternal reality of all these stories, this princess lavish with palms. She is gliding, or then it is you gliding near me along the paths of nightlight. Scarcely have we entered than all the little geniuses of childhood throw themselves around our necks. From a little transforming flower, our very learned guide Mr. Bolinaga, presiding over the development of all this display, did not, in fact, disdain to have the rabbit from *Alice in Wonderland* leap forth under our eyes, and it is Alice's dinner table unrolling as far as the eye can reach before us when we had raised to our mouth the lilliputian tomato of *pitanga,* with the exquisite taste of poison. Here is the long pointed leaf, darted with silk, which she must have used for her messages: it is impossible to write more distinctly with ink than on this silvery Japanese vellum. There would not even be any need to rip it off in order to cover it with characters, for it could share this fate with all the other like leaves without the low plant to which it belongs giving up its life. Think of what an exorbitant present that would be: bursting forth from a rather small earth pot, a love letter written in this way. . . After this living leaf to which we just saw Alice confide her projects, it would be impossible that another leaf should not rise before long, this one dried, but like a large ace of spades without a base, cut out in the cricket's wing: these must be her memories. It is difficult in quite another sense to snatch oneself away from the contemplation of this autochthonous species, I think, of *sempervivum* which enjoys the frightening property of continuing to develop under any conditions whatever and just as well starting from a bit of a leaf as from a leaf: crumpled, pierced, torn, burned, imprisoned between the pages of a book always closed, this glaucous scale—about which you cannot decide if it would be better finally to press it against your heart or to insult it—still endures. It tries, at the price of whatever revolting efforts, to reconstruct itself according to the destroyed probabilities that it has. It is lovely and confusing like human subjectivity, so that it comes forth more or less haggard from egalitarian revolutions. It is no less lovely, no less ineradicable than today's currently desperate will that can be termed *surrealist* just as well in the domain of particular sciences as in the domain of poetry and arts, operating at each moment the synthesis of the rational and the real, without fearing to place in the word "real" everything irrational it can contain *until further notice*. It is no lovelier, it is no poorer in reasons to be and no richer in becoming than separation in love, no matter how brief, than this delicious wound which opens and closes over a phosphorescent and secular series of temptations and dangers.

I forgot that, to ward off any wish on the part of *sempervivum* to invade the earth, men have found nothing better—that is to say, nothing else at all—than to boil it.

As, after a long sea voyage, the passengers about to disembark question the surprising pieces of silver and gold that will be the currency, there appears a dream country, Orotava, into which you are introduced by taking these leaves in your hand, the overwhelming coinage of feeling. Because it is here, on this side of the ocean, within the confines of a park, in a relatively closed vessel (if I judge by the outside) but set on the slope of an endless hope as soon as I entered there with you—as if I had just been transported to the very heart of the world—not only have the natural and the artificial succeeded in finding a perfect equilibrium, but in addition, there are electively united all the conditions of free extension and mutual tolerance that permit the harmonious gathering of individuals of a whole kingdom. We will never again be done with this foliage of the Golden Age. Orpheus has passed this way, pulling after him the tiger and the gazelle side by side. The heavy snakes uncoil and drop around the circular bench on which we sat to enjoy the deep dusk which finds the way to share the garden, at noon, with the broad daylight. This bench, surrounding a tree several meters across, I am burning to call it the bench of fever. The poisonous smell pierces the intervals of the slippery skins which, without leaving the tree, plunge into the ground to spring up again some distance away in terrible arches. All that remains of the light seems produced only by the far-off lamps, too white in color, of the *datura*, seen through the sparse chains of the crisscross pattern. The quality of this light makes it less bearable than would be its absence in such a place. You think you see evening dresses hanging in the air, dazzling in their pallor. In the depths of the day or the night, no matter which, it's something like the immense vestibule of physical love as one would wish to make it without interruption. The curtains drawn, the bars twisted, the caressing feline eyes alone streaking the sky. Delirium of absolute presence. How could one not find oneself wishing to love like this, in the bosom of reconciled nature? Nevertheless they are there, all the interdictions, the alarm bells, all ready to be set off, the snowy bells of the *datura* in case we might decide to place this insuperable barrier between the others and ourselves. Love, only love that you are, carnal love, I adore, I have never ceased to adore your lethal shadow, your mortal shadow. A day will come where man will be able to recognize you for his only master, honoring you even in the mysterious perversions you surround him with. On this bench, learning from the mangrove, I know perfectly well that I am only this man as a child; I have not yet succeeded in obtaining from the genius of beauty that it be just the same, with its bright or dark wings, that it should shine resplendent for me under both these aspects at once in what I love. The child I still am in relation to what I should like to be has not quite unlearned the dualism of good and evil. These roots half in the air, half under the ground, these vines, these indiscernible snakes, this mixture of seduction and fear, he could not swear it didn't resemble for him Bluebeard's beard. But you, Ondine, still accompanying me, I had a presentiment of your alburnum eyes without ever having seen their like. I love you in spite of Bluebeard's beard[1] and by the diamond of the Canary Island air right in the face as it forms a single bouquet of everything which grows jealously alone here and there over the earth's surface. I love you so that I lose myself in the illusion that a window either too opaque or too transparent has been opened in a petal of the *datura,* that I am alone here under the tree, and that at a signal wonderfully awaited I shall go to join you in the fascinating and fatal flower.

The perfect self-sufficiency that love between two beings tends to cause finds no obstacle at this moment. The sociologist should perhaps pay it some notice, he who, under Europe's sky, only goes so far as to turn his gaze, fogged in by the smoky and roaring mouth of factories, toward the fearfully obstinate peace of the fields. This has not ceased, and perhaps it is more than ever the time to remember that this self-sufficiency is one of the goals of human activity; that economic and psychological speculations, no matter how inimical to each other they seem today, revolve about it in a remarkable manner. Engels, in *The Origin of the Family,* does not hesitate to make of *individual sexual love,* born of this *superior form of sexual relations that monogamy is, the greatest moral progress* accomplished by humans in modern times. Whatever twist is given to Marxist thought today on this point as on so many others, it is undeniable that the authors of the *Communist Manifesto* never ceased to protest any return to the "disordered" sexual relations which marked the dawn of human history. Once private property has been abolished, "we can reasonably affirm," declares Engels, "that *far from disappearing, monogamy will be realized for the first time.*" In the same work he insists several times on the *exclusive* character of this love which, at the price of whatever deviations—I know some miserable ones and some grandiose ones—has finally *found* itself. This view about what might be thought the most exciting topic related to human becoming is nowhere more clearly corroborated than by the view of Freud, for whom sexual love, even such as it is already presented, *breaks the collective links created by race, rises above national differences and social hierarchies, and, in so doing, contributes in large measure to the progress of culture.* These two testimonies, which present a conception, less and less frivolous, of love as a fundamental principle for moral as well as cultural progress, would seem to me by themselves of such a nature as to give poetic activity a major role as a tried and tested means to fix the sensitive and moving world on a single being as well as a permanent force of anticipation.

Try to speak, they will tell me, of the self-sufficiency of love to those in the grip of implacable necessity, which leaves them just enough time to breathe and sleep! *L'Age d'or:* for me these words, which crossed my mind as I began to surrender to the inebriating shades of Orotava, remain associated with a few unforgettable images of the film of Buñuel and Dali which had appeared formerly under this title and with which, precisely, Benjamin Péret and I would have acquainted the public of the Canaries in 1935, if Spanish censorship had not chosen so rapidly to show itself even more intolerant than French censorship. This film remains, to this day, the only enterprise of exaltation of total love such as I envisage it,[2] and the violent reactions of its representations in Paris produced have only strengthened my consciousness of its incomparable value. Love, in everything it can contain for two beings, which is absolutely limited to them, isolated from the rest of the world, has never shown itself so freely, with so much tranquil audacity. The stupidity, the hypocrisy, the routine, can never keep such a work from having been born, or keep a man and a woman, on the screen, from inflicting on the entire world as it rises against them the spectacle of an exemplary love. In such a love there exists potentially a veritable *golden age* in complete rupture with the age of mud Europe is going through and of a richness inexhaustible with *future* possibilities. I have always been glad Buñuel and Dali stress this, and I feel a deep melancholy at the thought that Buñuel changed his mind afterwards about this title, that, upon the insistence of a few tawdry revolutionaries determined to submit everything to their immediate propaganda goals, he consented to have shown in the workers' movie houses an expurged vision of *L'Age d'or* that someone had suggested to him to entitle, to be completely within the rules, "In the Frozen Waters of Egotistic Calculation." I shall not be cruel enough to insist on what there might be that is childishly reassuring for some in the labelling, by means of one part of a sentence of Marx drawn from the first pages of the *Manifesto,* of a production as irreducible as *L'age d'or* on the scale of the *present* human demands. On the other hand, I protest with all my strength against the ambiguity introduced by this title, an ambiguity which must have escaped Buñuel but which was likely to please those who most despise his thought and mine also. "In the Frozen Waters of Egotistic Calculations": it was obviously all too easy to have that mean—scorning Marx's context, but never mind—that it is love that tends to plunge us into those frozen waters; that we must have done, mustn't we, with this sort of love, a blazing challenge to a cynicism more and more general, an insult to the physical and moral impotence of today. Certainly not! Never, *for any reason,* shall I pass over to that way of thinking. In spite of everything, I shall continue to maintain that "in the frozen waters of egotistic calculation" is perhaps everywhere, except where there is *this* love. Too bad if that offends the mockers and scoundrels. Who would dare to speak here of calculation, who would refuse, supposing it is kept, to take the word "egotistic" applied to love in its philosophic sense and thus only in this sense, without anything pejorative about it any longer. The recreation, the perpetual recoloration of the world in a single being, such as they are accomplished through love, light up with a thousand rays the advance of the earth ahead. Each time a person loves, nothing can prevent everyone's feelings being involved. In order not to let them down, the involvement must be entire.

On a very general level, concern with material necessity frustrates love as well as poetry, in concentrating all the human attention that should be available on the problem of subsistence. This concern has proved itself, along the way, so pressing as to leave no room for any other in the minds of some of my friends. In Orotava it gives way to the most beautiful of childhood's mirages. I was quite astonished, in the time when we were just beginning to practice automatic writing, at the frequency with which the words *tree for bread, tree for butter,* and so on, tended to recur in our texts.[3] Quite recently, I was wondering if we shouldn't detect in the strange fascination that these words hold for children the secret of the technical discovery that seems to have put Raymond Roussel in possession of the very keys of the imagination: "I chose a word then linked it to another by the preposition *for.*" The preposition in question seems in fact to be by far the most rapid and certain vehicle to transport the image. I will add that it is enough to link in that way *no matter what* noun to *no matter what* other one for a world of new representations to surge up immediately. In any case the bread tree or the butter tree dominate by their whole verifiable existence the innumerable creations that can thus be obtained. What is so appealing about the idea of them when you are very young has to do with their reconciling particularly well the pleasure principle with the reality principle. One myth among all the others, clear and without harshness, is developed starting with this tree: that of the inexhaustible natural generosity able to see to the most diverse human needs. The very air is suddenly composed of the trembling of veils of a thousand imponderable Virginias.[4] How to resist the charm of a garden like this one, where all the trees of a providential type have gathered? In this place the great moral and other constructions of grown men, founded as they are on the glorification of effort, of heavy labor, are endangered. Livelihood we call "earned" returns to the aspect it had for us in childhood: it takes on once more the character of a life wasted. Wasted for games, wasted for love. What is required most earnestly to keep up this sort of life loses all its value at the passage of the great dream trees, each of which declines for man an immeasurable quality included in the very syllables of its name. The bread tree, the butter tree have called to them the salt tree, the pepper tree: a whole frugal lunch is being improvised. How hungry we are! The traveler tree and the soap tree are going to let us present ourselves at the table with clean hands. I think this must be the Good Inn Rimbaud speaks of. [5] From immensely high beams the long smoked fruits of the prodigious sausage tree are hanging. On one side, the great imperial fig tree reigns imperiously over all the expressions of strange life in this setting. Its roots climb up to the very top like a procession of little balloons, which, depending on their exposure to the sun, takes on all colors of the sea anemone. This strange life of the imperial fig tree is so forceful that, I was told, a few years ago a visitor could be seen running to encounter it, unscrupulously trampling all the flowerbeds and showing all the signs of mental disorder: when inquiries were made, it was only a mycologist from Europe who thought he had discovered a new species of mushroom. —What is strangest is inseparable from love, presiding over its revelation in individual as well as in collective terms. Man's and woman's sexual organs are attracted to each other like a magnet only through the introduction between them of a web of uncertainties ceaselessly renewed, a real unloosing of hummingbirds which would have gone to hell to have their feathers smoothed. Once the problem of human material life is supposedly resolved, as I am playing at believing it resolved within this framework, I immediately run into these startling uncertainties, and for an instant I want to look at them only. My love for you has only increased since the first day: under the imperial fig tree it trembles and laughs in the sparks of all its daily forges. Because you are unique, you can't help being for me always another, another you. Across the diversity of these inconceivable flowers over there, it is you over there changing whom I love in a red blouse, naked, in a gray blouse.

From this impassioned landscape which will withdraw some day soon with the sea, if I have to take only you from the phantasmagoria of the green foam, I shall know how to recreate this music over our steps. These steps make an infinite border for the meadow we have to cross in order to come back, the magical meadow circling the fig tree's empire. I discover in myself no other treasure than the key which opens for me this limitless meadow ever since I have known you, this meadow made from the repetition of a single plant always taller, whose increasing span will carry me to my death. Death, whence the grandfather clock bedecked with country flowers, as beautiful as my tombstone stood on its end, will start up again on tiptoe to sing the hours not passing. For a woman and a man, who, to the end of time, must be you and me, will glide along, when it is their turn, without ever looking back, as far as the path leads, in the oblique light, at the edge of life and of the oblivion of life, in the delicate grass running before us to its arborescence. It is composed, this lacy grass, of a thousand invisible, unbreakable links, which happen to chain your nervous system with mine in the deepest night of knowledge. This ship, rigged by hands of children, exhausts the bobbin of fate. It is this grass which will continue after me to line the walls of the humblest room each time two lovers enclose themselves, scorning everything that can happen, even the approach of the end of their lives. No rock, no matter how high it reaches, no rock threatening to fall each second, can keep this grass from becoming so dense around the bed as to hide the rest of the world from the two gazes seeking each other and losing each other. The traces of whitewashing, the chipped bowl, the tatters, the poor chair, rolled by the endless sea of my grass, will never cede anything to the impeccable settings, the luxurious costumes. Nothing is worth exchanging for it, and nothing would have any more value if it were to change. The greatest hope, I say, the one in which all the others are met, is that it exists for everyone and that for everyone it lasts. That the absolute gift of one being to another, which can exist only in reciprocity, be in the eyes of everyone the only natural and supernatural hanging bridge cast across life itself. But then what is this enigmatic grass, by turns that of foresting and that of total deforesting, this foliage of the mimosa of your eyes? Rumor has it, lighter than a wave crossing over it, that it is the *sensitive plant.*[6]

We will never have done with sensation. All rationalist systems will prove one day to be indefensible to the extent that they try, if not to reduce it to the extreme, at least not to consider it in its so-called exaggerations. These exaggerations are, and we have to admit it, what most interest the poet. The struggle between the partisans of the "resolution" method, as they say in scientific language, and the partisans of the "invention" method has never been so heated as today, and everything seems to indicate that there is no way out. I think I have shown no more pessimism than anyone else about the advance of a thought which, completely independent, remains consequent without repeating itself. But truth obliges me to say that this thought, left to its own devices, has always seemed to me to oversimplify; that, far from satisfying me, it has frustrated in me the taste for everything that it is not, the taste for the great ups and downs in terrain or in other things, which at least temporarily make difficulties for it. This is the *surrealist* attitude as it has always been defined. I am assured that it is shared today by all categories of thinkers. I am not the one to say it—rather, Juvet, in *The Structure of New Physical Theories,* written in 1933: "It is in the surprise created by a new image or by a new association of images, that we have to see the most important element of progress in the physical sciences, because astonishment excites logic, always rather cold, obliging it to establish new coordinates." That is sufficient to crush all those who challenge us, incriminating the road we are claiming to follow as too adventurous. They are saying—what aren't they saying!—that the world has nothing strange to offer where we are, are claiming it just *changed* like the voice of a young boy; they object lugubriously that the time of fairy stories is over. Over for them! If I want the world to change, if I even mean to consecrate part of my own life to its changing in its social aspect, it is not in the vain hope of returning to the time of these stories, but of course, in the hope of helping the time to come when they will no longer just be stories. Surprise must be sought for itself, unconditionally. It exists only in the interweaving in a single object of the natural and the supernatural, in the emotion of holding the lyrebird even as it is felt to be slipping away. To see natural necessity opposing human or logical necessity, no longer to try desperately to reconcile them, to deny in love the persistence of falling in love and, in life, the perfect continuity of the impossible and the possible—these are tantamount to acknowledging the loss of what I maintain is the only state of grace.

A contact which wasn't even that for us, an involuntary contact with a single branch of the sensitive plant causes the meadow to shudder outside as inside us. We have nothing to do with it, or very little, and yet the whole expanse of grass bends down. It's a regulated slaughter like that of a snowball hurled in full sunlight at a set of snow skittles. Or then a drum roll which, suddenly, would unite all the companies of partridges in the world. I need just to touch you for the quicksilver of the sensitive plant to bend its harp upon the horizon. But provided we stop a moment, the grass will turn green again, will be born again, after which my new steps will have no other goal than to reinvent you. I shall reinvent you for me, since I desire to see poetry and life recreated perpetually. From one branch to the other of the sensitive plant—without any fear of violating the laws of space and braving all kinds of anachronisms—I like to think that a warning, subtle and certain, from the tropics to the North Pole, goes on its way as from the beginning of the world to its other pole. I accept, on my own path, the discovery that I am only its insignificant cause. All that matters is the universal, eternal effect: I exist only insofar as it is reversible in my direction.

Oratava is no more, gradually disappearing above us, just now engulfed, or then, these fifteen hundred meters high, we have just been swallowed by a cloud. Here we are at the unformed interior, prey to the hasty notion, inexplicably satisfying for humans, of something that can be "cut with a knife." This cloud blinds me, only generating more clouds in my mind. Baudelaire, at the end of the first poem of the *Paris Spleen*, seems only to have multiplied the suspension points: "I love the clouds. . . the clouds passing. . . over there. . . over there. . . the marvelous clouds!" so that clouds would really pass by before our eyes, appearing like suspension points between the earth and the sky. In fact, looking at a cloud from the earth is really the best way to interrogate one's own desire. To put it in vulgar terms, we are wrong to think that we are exhausting the meaning of a famous dramatic scene, smiling with pity when poor Polonius, fearing to displease Hamlet, is willing to consent to a cloud having the shape of a camel. . . or a weasel. . . or a whale. I think we should take up this passage in a completely different spirit, its true sense being the discovery of the deep psychological motives for Hamlet's behavior during the whole play. It is certainly not at random that the names of these three animals, and not others, come to his lips. The sudden trigger that marks the passage from one to the other tells us a lot about the paroxystic nervousness of the hero. If we know how to look at it, it is more than probable that this animal form, in three successive aspects, would appear as rich in hidden meaning as that of the vulture discovered by Oscar Pfister in the famous Saint Anne of the Louvre, subject of the admirable piece by Freud called "A Childhood Memory of Leonardo da Vinci." The flabbiness of Polonius, had it not been so strongly stressed before, would not appear in his answers about the cloud. Leonardo, inviting his students to copy their paintings from what they would see (remarkably arranged and appropriate for each one of them) when they stared at an old wall for a period of time, is still far from being understood. The whole problem of the passage from subjectivity to objectivity is implicitly resolved there, and the implications of this resolution are fuller of human interest than those of a simple technique, even if the technique were that of inspiration itself. It is particularly in this way that it held the interest of *surrealism*. Surrealism did not start with this technique, but rather found it along its way, and with it, its possibilities for extending to all the domains beyond painting. The novel associations of images that the poet, the artist, the scholar bring forth are comparable in that they take some grid[7] of a particular texture, whether this texture be concretely that of a decrepit wall, of a cloud, or of anything else: some prolonged and vague sound carries this melody that we needed to hear, excluding any other. What is most striking is that an activity of this kind which, in order to be, requires the unconditional acceptance of a more or less lasting passivity, far from limiting itself to the world of the senses, has been able to attain, in depth, the moral world. The luck, the fortune of the scholar or the artist when they *find* can only be thought of as a particular case of human luck; it cannot be distinguished from that in its essence. A person will know how to proceed when, like the painter, he consents to reproduce, without any change, what an appropriate grid tells him in advance of his own acts. This grid exists. Every life contains these homogenous patterns of facts, whose surface is cracked or cloudy. Each person has only to stare at them fixedly in order to read his own future. Let him enter the whirlwind; let him retrace the events which have seemed to him fleeting and obscure among all others, which have torn him apart. There – if his questioning is worth it – all the logical principles, having been routed, will bring him the strength of that *objective chance* which makes a mockery of what would have seemed most probable. Everything humans might want to know is written upon this grid in phosphorescent letters, in letters of *desire*.

The purely visual exercise of the faculty that used to be called the "paranoiac" way of looking permitted the observation that even if the same spot, on the wall or anywhere else, is almost always interpreted differently by two individuals with their distinct desires, it does not follow that one of them cannot rather easily have the other perceive what he sees in it. There seems to be no *a priori* reason for this primary illusion not to roam the world. It will suffice for it to correspond to the most insistent and penetrating vision, in that it must potentially put into play the greatest possible number of *optical remainders*. If only you try to find out the reactions of the average man, you notice that he is not at all lacking in the faculty of paranoiac interpretation, although it is usually still in an uncultivated state. But he is ready, and willing, to agree with the interpretation proposed to him, behaving in this like Polonius: even better, if he has kept some freshness of feeling, he takes a candid pleasure in sharing another's illusion. Therein resides a deep source of communication between beings that has only to be disengaged from everything that is likely to unsettle or overlay it. Real objects do not exist just as they are: looking at the lines that make up the most common among them, you see surging forth – without even having to blink—a remarkable *riddle-image* which is identical with it and which speaks to us, without any possible mistake, of the only *real* object, the actual one of our *desire*. Needless to say, what is true of the complementary graphic image in question is no less true of a certain verbal image upon which any poetry worthy of the name has never ceased to call. Such images, whose best examples are found in Lautréamont, are endowed with a persuasive strength rigorously proportional to the violence of the initial shock they produced. Thus it is that close up, they are destined to take on the character of things *revealed*. Once again, acts themselves, those acts to be accomplished, must be imperatively set in relief against the mass of the acts already accomplished from the time that we can consider this mass, whether that of a wall or a cloud, with *indifference*. From the time when we shall have found the way of freeing ourselves at will from every logical or moral preoccupation.

Desire, the only motive of the world, desire, the only rigor humans must be acquainted with, where could I be better situated to adore it than on the inside of the cloud? The forms that the clouds take, as they are seen from the ground, are in no way random; they are, rather, augural. If a good part of modern psychology tends to stress that fact, I am all the more certain that Baudelaire sensed its coming in that stanza of "Voyage" where the last line echoes the first three so oddly, charging them with meaning:

> Les plus riches cités, les plus grands paysages
> Jamais ne contenaient l'attrait mystérieux
> De ceux que le hasard fait avec les nuages
> Et toujours le désir nous rendait soucieux!
>
> (None of the famous landscapes that we saw
> equalled the mysterious allure

of those that chance arranges in the clouds . . .
And our desire would let us have no peace!)[8]

Here I am in the cloud, here in the intensely opaque room I've always dreamed of penetrating. I wander in the superb bathroom of vapor. Everything around me is unknown to me. Surely somewhere there is a chest of drawers with astounding boxes on its shelves. I am walking on cork. How mad they must have been to stand a mirror in all this debris! And the faucets spitting out the steam! Supposing there are faucets. I am looking for you. Even your voice has been taken away by the fog. The chill sends an emery board over my nails, ninety meters long (at a hundred I will have no nails left). I desire you. I desire only you. I caress the white bears without reaching you. No other woman will ever have access to this room where you are a thousand, as I decompose all the gestures I have seen you make. Where are you? I am playing hide and seek with ghosts. But I will certainly end up finding you, and the whole world will be newly lit from our loving each other, because a chain of illuminations passes through us. Because it takes in a multitude of couples who like us will know forever how to make a diamond from the white night. I am this man with the sea urchin lashes who for the first time raises his eyes on the woman who must be everything for him, in a blue street. In the evening this terribly poor man, embracing for the first time a woman on a bridge who will never again be able to tear herself away from him. I am, in the clouds, this man who, to reach the one he loves, is condemned to displace a pyramid made of her garments.

A great festival wind blowing; the swings have started their motion again; scarcely have I had the time to see the seafoam bath rise again to the highest snows, the admirable chrome apparatus return to the bed of the torrent. In the sun are drying as many bath wraps as the times your image was repeated in the misty room. These are the violently odorous tablecloths of the flowers of a white broom, the *retama,* the only shrub growing at this height. It clings to the calcified and cracking shell of the earth with its magnificent benches curled round with white mussels skipping down towards the arid and deserted south of the island. On this side, the risks of landslide have led the natives to raise stone fences which wed the slightest natural folds, conferring a terraced look, cellular and empty, disturbing on a wide stretch of landscape. From the blond to the brunette, the earth exhausts for the eye all the shades of honey. Up above, an immobile kite bird, its wings spread out, seems to have been there since the beginning of time, proclaiming the impossibility of there being any life among these rocks. Any life, if I except that of the *retama,* which, in the best-sheltered angle of each polygon, curls its flowers in profusion. It is the first time that I have felt, before the *never yet seen,* such a complete impression of the *already seen.*[9] This strange partition, this light of a heap of sand, these faded helixes lying around as after a great feast of praying mantises, and, above all, this single flowering which one might be likely to take for the radiant seething of destruction, but of course: these are, such as he invented them two months before we left for the Canary Islands, these are the "airplane-swallowing gardens" of Max Ernst. Then your life and mine were already turning around these gardens whose existence he could not have suspected and towards whose discovery he set off each morning, always more handsome under his kite-bird mask.

There is no sophism more deadly than the one that consists in presenting the accomplishment of the sexual act as being necessarily accompanied by a falling-off of amorous potential between two

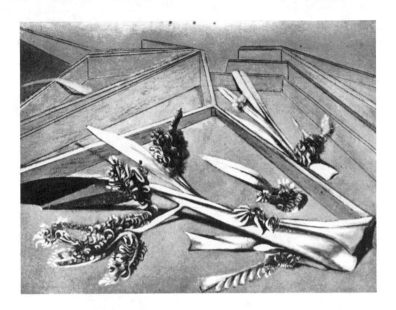

beings, a falling-off which, repeating, would lead them progressively to no longer suffice for each other. In that way, love would lay itself open to ruin, to the very extent to which it pursued its own realization. A still denser shadow would descend upon life, in a mass proportional to each new explosion of light. Here a human being would be destined to lose, little by little, its elective affinity for another; it would be brought back unwilling to its essence. It would be extinguished some day, a victim of its own radiance. The great nuptial flight would provoke the more or less slow combustion of one being in the eyes of the other, a combustion at the end of which, as other creatures would garb themselves in mystery and charm for each of them, they would all be free to make a new choice when they had redescended to the earth. Nothing is more insensitive, more depressing than this conception. I know of none more widespread and thereby more capable of representing the present world as a great misery. So Juliet, continuing to live, would no longer be always *more* Juliet for Romeo! It is easy to separate out the two fundamental errors that preside over such an attitude: one a social cause, the other a moral one. The social error, to which there is no other remedy than the destruction of the very economical bases of present society, resides in the fact that the initial choice in love is not *really* allowed, that, to the very extent that it tends to impose itself as an exception, it evolves in an atmosphere of non-choice which is hostile to its triumph. The sordid considerations that are set up against it, the underhanded war made upon it, even more, the violently antagonistic representations abundant around it, always ready to attack, are, it must be admitted, readily discouraging. But this love, *the bearer of the greatest hopes that have been translated into art for centuries,* I am hard-pressed to see what could stop it from winning out in conditions of life as they might be renewed. The moral error that, concurrent with the former one, leads us to represent love, in its lasting, as a declining phenomenon resides in the incapacity of most people, even in love, to free themselves from any preoccupation foreign to it, from every fear as from every doubt, exposing themselves without defense to the overwhelming gaze of the god. Here experience, artistic as well as scientific, comes to the rescue, proving that everything that is built and remains has first required this abandon just in order to *be*. Nothing could be more worth an effort than making love lose this bitter aftertaste which poetry, for example, does not have. Such an enterprise cannot be entirely successful until on the universal scale we have finished with the infamous Christian idea of sin. There has never been any forbidden fruit. Only temptation is divine. To feel the need to vary the object of this temptation, to replace it by others— this bears witness that one is about to be found unworthy, that one has already doubtless proved unworthy of *innocence*. From innocence in the sense of absolute nonguilt. If really the choice was free, it cannot be the one who made it who contests it, under any pretext. Guilt starts from that and not from anything else. I reject here the excuse of habit, of weariness. Reciprocal love, such as I envisage it, is a system of mirrors which reflects for me, under the thousand angles that the unknown can take for me, the faithful image of the one I love, always more surprising in her divining of my own desire and more gilded with life.

Here it is hard to tell if it is for entering or for leaving that the door of the circus of mists opens so often. The immense tent is marvelously patched by daylight. So it is easy to establish a perfect continuity between what is opened and what is veiled. It is no different in the kind of love where desire carried to the extreme appears to bloom just in order to sweep its lighthouse beam over the always new clearings of life. No depression follows upon joy. The room filled with swandown which we were just now crossing, and which we will cross again, communicates effortlessly with nature. Speckling with blue and gold the reefs of honey devoid of any living being, I see a thousand eyes of children watching the summit that we will not be able to reach. It must be about time to set up the trapeze.

The sublime imagination, linked to a philosophical conscience of the first order, has invented nothing so great as the episode of the Marquis de Sade's *New Justine* which has Mt. Etna as a background: "Looking at Etna one day, with its breast vomiting forth flames, I wanted to be this famous volcano. . ." I remind the reader that the invocation to Etna, pronounced meanwhile, has the result of making the chemist Almani emerge from the shadows to lay his formidable science at the service of the hero. Guided by their common hatred of nature and of men—rigorously protesting that love of nature and of primitive man that so exalts the work of Rousseau—Jerome and Almani take as their duty the perpetuation of evil in strict collaboration with nature. To be sure, man no longer unites with nature except in crime: it remains a question if that is not still a way, one of the maddest, one of the most unarguable, to love it. This Almani, who means to stand in opposition, trait for trait, to "the lover of nature," who declares himself the executioner of nature, why then does he find such pleasure in mixing his sperm with the burning flow of lava? I know no other words assembled with such genius, words whose composition is capable of provoking an emotion so intense and so durable as those which, having reached this point in his tale, Sade cast on the wind of the little sheets of his manuscript that seem to constitute the project of the work: "The secret for bringing into being an earthquake." But more admirable still is the fact that this secret was delivered—militant anarchy, as it cannot, after all, be overcome because it expresses one of the most pathetic sides of human nature, has no more stirring letters of nobility—that we attend the superficial burial of innumerable loaves of bread from twenty to forty pounds each, kneaded with water, with filings, and with sulphur, placed not far from each other and destined, as they warm up in the earth, to provoke a new eruption, an eruption all the lovelier in that nature only went along this time, that it is a human who willed it. "The procedure," says Sade, "was easy." How could we overlook the heart-rending humor in this confession? Never, I say, has terrestrial magnetism, responsible for placing one of the poles of the magnet in the mind of man and the other in nature, been so implacably revealed. Making sure that in any case this magnetism exists permits us, up to a certain point, to overlook the question of whether or not the two poles have contrary signs, or the same one.

The problem of evil is worth discussing only until we have finished with the idea of the transcendency of some good or other which could dictate to man his duty. Until that time, the exalted representation of an innate "evil" will retain the greatest revolutionary value. Beyond that, I hope that man will be able to adopt with respect to nature a less haggard attitude than simply passing from adoration to horror. That, turning with all the greater curiosity towards it, he will manage to think of it more or less what Goethe thought of one of his contemporaries when he said: "Do I love or hate Wieland? – I don't know. – At heart I care about him."

Nature is likely to light up and to fade out, to serve and not to serve me, only to the extent that I feel the rise and the fall of the fire of a hearth which is love, the only love, that for a *single* being. I have known, in the absence of this love, the real skies empty, the flotsam of everything I was about to grasp in the Dead Sea, the desert of flowers. Did nature betray me? No, I felt that the principle of its devastation was in me. It was only lacking for a great iris of fire to emerge from me to give its value to what exists. How beautiful everything becomes in the light of the fire! The least shard of glass finds a way of being at once blue and rose. From this upper landing of the Teide, where the eye sees no slight blade of grass, where everything might appear so frozen and so dark, I contemplate to the point of dizziness your hands opened above the fire of twigs which we just kindled and which is now raging, your enchanting hands, your transparent hands hovering over the fire of my life.

Wonderful Teide, take my life! Turn, under those radiant hands and make all my facets sparkle. I want to make only one being with your flesh, the very flesh of the medusas, for one single being alone to be the medusa of the seas of desire. Mouth of the heavens and yet mouth of hell, I prefer you thus in your enigma, able to send natural beauty to the skies and to swallow up everything. It is my heart beating in your inviolable depths, in this blinding rose garden of mathematical folly where you mysteriously ready your power. May your arteries, traversed with beautiful, vibrant black blood, guide me at length towards everything I have to know, to love, toward everything that must make a plume at the end of my fingers! Let my thoughts speak through you, through the thousand screeching mouths of the ermines where you display yourself at sunrise! You truly bear the floral ark which would no longer be the ark were you not to hold above it the single branch of lightning; you mingle with my love; this love and you are destined as far as the eye can reach to create the dust of diamonds. The great bottomless lakes of light succeed in me with the rapid passing of your exhalations. From you all roads to the infinite, all springs, all the lightbeams leap, Deria-i-Noor and Koh-i-Noor, lovely crest of a single diamond trembling!

On the side of the abyss, made of philosophers' stone, the starry castle opens.

6 Fable has it that, in spite of the dress woven by the Graces, Venus was wounded by Diomedes. The vulnerability of the goddess is put in specific terms. Love, in what is most earthly about it—Venus endangered herself in order to defend Aeneas, the son she had from the most backward man, the shepherd—has to be touched during the course of life in its flesh, and the myth writer was careful to specify, in their ineluctable linking, the facts that are to bring about this passing mortification. At their origin Eris, or Discord, rages, engraving on the golden apple the fateful inscription: "To the most beautiful."

Before the force of such a myth, witnessed to by its immediate spreading and its lasting until our time, we cannot have any doubt about its expression of a common eternal truth, that it translates into allegorical language a series of proved observations that could have no other domain than human existence. For indeed passion, with its magnificent wild eyes, must suffer at having to mix in the human struggle. One must admit that even when it is the surest of itself, it may occasionally trip up in the corridor of minutes, hours, days following each other and *not being alike*. This corridor, with variable stars above it, is successively inundated with light, crepuscular, or totally dark. In the minor shadows, completely exterior to passion, there await, to stop it in its path, materiality and intellectuality, in the very terms of the Greek story—Juno and Minerva—her supplanted rivals and principal enemies.

How cruel and lovely is this myth of Venus! From a dead love

*On the side of the abyss, made
of philosophers' stone . . .* (p.97

there can only arise the springtime of an anemone. It is at the price of a wound required by the adversary powers who control man that living love triumphs.

Whether or not it results from the conjunction of Venus with Mars at a particular place in the sky of my birth, I have all too often felt the bad effects of discord in the very inside of love. That is, moreover, a banal theme of popular songs. Discord makes a rapid appearance between the lovers: nothing could have predicted it, for that would have naturally made it easy to disarm. I have been able to convince myself, at a distance, that it almost always came in through some caprice of one or the other, a caprice which, for purely circumstantial reasons, may confront entirely different dispositions. Perhaps a life lived totally in common by two beings who love each other renders this kind of incident inevitable. Nonetheless, it is always with surprise and fright that I have seen, in such a case, the harmless complaints that take their pretext in this state of things grow more acute. They hone themselves on the stone of *silence,* abrupt and unbreakable by anything at all, quite like absence and death. Overhead heads, then between the lovers, flies a rain of poisoned arrows, soon so thick as to prevent any exchange of glances. Then hastily, hateful egoism walls itself into a windowless tower. The attraction is broken; even the loveliness of the beloved face goes into hiding; a wind of ashes sweeps everything away; the pursuit of life is compromised. Needless to say, these instants are counted, being at the mercy of any sign of understanding – some involuntary relaxing, some familiar gesture – in order to end without leaving the slightest trace. Venus, because she wanted to interfere in human war, was wounded in the hand, that is, momentarily paralyzed in her very action. Beyond that, she becomes herself again and puts her magic belt back on.

These black moments when love suddenly flutters its wings and droops lifelessly into the abyss, whence it will rise up again afterwards in a straight line—I think we should consider them face to face and fearlessly to the extent that, in an appropriate behavior, they can be limited within the framework of human life. It is particularly important to know how to judge a sudden incompatibility revealed between two lovers: does this incompatibility take in the deep causes which have sapped the foundations of love for a long time or is it just the product of a series of arbitrary, unrelated causes? I am not interested in the first case, for I am writing *Mad Love*. In the second case, where I put myself, I say that these occasional causes have to be brought to light, without our being put off either by their entangling, nor, in the last analysis, by the highly enigmatic character of some of them. Given the violence of the shock which, when they had no way of expecting it, sets into discord two beings who were until that moment in perfect accord and who, at the first clearing, tomorrow or very soon, will not be able to understand their own reflexes, given all the anguish and its gigantic constructions of cardboard in the style of termite dwellings which, quicker than you can bat an eyelash, replace everything, it seems to me that we are in the presence of an evil sufficiently definite for us to decide to uncover its origins, which should permit us to find an eventual remedy. It is a matter, as I said, of ruling against the widespread opinion that love wears out, like the diamond, in its own dust and that this dust hangs suspended during our life. If it can be proved that love may emerge intact from such error, it is doubtless not the same for the loving being. This being is susceptible to suffering, and worse still, to misunderstanding the cause of suffering. Because of the absolute gift of himself, he is tempted to incriminate love in a case when it is only life that is at fault.

Examining closely one of these "faults" in life, I have recently been able to persuade myself that, far from answering the idea one normally has of a natural risk—an icy road, a hole—presented the characteristics of a *trap*. I mean that it was prepared by something ingenious and sure which at least in part goes beyond my present understanding and which, by that very fact, was to make my fall inevitable.

On July 20, 1936, about three in the afternoon, the bus had set us both down near a little beach on the outskirts of Lorient: the Blocked-Fort. We hadn't chosen to go there rather than elsewhere: we had left with the first bus. The weather was still "threatening," as it had been since our arrival in Brittany, except in the days of tempest and of rain. Less than a week earlier we had already let ourselves be led towards this place on the coast, where, given the conditions, no one seemed to be venturing but ourselves. This first time, rapidly bored with contemplating a dismal stretch of sand and pebbles, we had had no other imaginative recourse than to start looking for the small and scarce objects washed up upon it. Gathered, they were not without a certain charm: a few small electric light bulbs, some blue bits of driftwood, a champagne cork, remnants of a pink candle, a cuttlefish bone no less pink, a little round metallic candy box inscribed with the word "violet," a tiny crab skeleton marvelously intact and chalk-white which seemed to me the lily of the valley of the sun, today unseen, in the Cancer constellation. All these elements could have formed one of those object-talismans surrealism still cares so much about. But, on July 20, it was all the less a matter of taking up that pastime again, since the sea, which had pulled back less of a distance, had manifestly left nothing at all unexpected behind it. It was the mournful repetition, too close in time, of a place especially banal and hostile for that banality itself, like all those that have nothing to say to our attention. This place could only be left behind as quickly as possible, by following the coastline because there was no other way of getting back.

I found walking along the dry sand without any determined goal rapidly discouraging. By asking around, we found that the first inhabited place we would come upon would be a little bathing station, Le Pouldu, about ten kilometers from Fort-Bloqué. As we gradually moved forward, the dismal nature of the site, which developed without changing in any sense, took on a poignant twist we could sense in our conversation, however increasingly vague. I remember, as I passed rather far from them, the singular irritation provoked in me by a bustling flock of seabirds squawking against a last ridge of foam. I even started throwing stones at them, but my gesture alone made them quiver in a single mass and sink farther on in their heavy flight. We walked along increasingly more separate without anything conscious having been decided on, except that I had preferred to walk on the ground along the shore to going barefooted. But this feeling of separation was not just an effect of physical distance: it did not in fact dissipate even when a barrier of rocks I could not cross brought us back side by side for a few steps. I have no trouble admitting that as far as I was concerned, I was in a progressively worse mood. On the land side, complete solitude, nothing that might signal the approach of a village. I walked with dismay over a carpet of dwarf heath and emaciated blue thistles bearing clusters of white snails. Would this day never end! The presence of an apparently uninhabited house a hundred meters along on the right added to the absurd and unjustifiable nature of our walking along in a setting like this. This house, recently built, had nothing to compensate the watching eye for its isolation. It opened out on a rather large enclosure stretching down to the sea and bordered, it seemed to me, by a metallic trellis, which, given the prodigious avarice of the land in such a place, had a lugubrious effect on me, without my stopping to analyze it. My gift of observation, which is in general not remarkable, was noticeably diminished by sadness. Consequently, I cannot at all account for the no less unfavorable impression made in me by the stream I next had to cross by a rather long detour, a stream that, before reaching the sea, flowed into a sort of quarry, rolling about rock-candy-colored water. In any case, it was the crossing of this fault—beyond which there stretched, as far as the eye could see, a landscape like the preceding one—that gave me the *panicked* desire to turn back on my steps: I was certain that it was late, that we had no hope of arriving before nightfall; if my opinion was not shared, I declared myself quite ready to return alone. I have rarely conducted myself in such an unreasonable manner. I nevertheless consented to ask the time from some workers engaged in some sort of work or other above the stream: it was not yet four-thirty. Having no further excuse to turn back, I started out again against my will. The rift between us was deeper still, as if by all the height of the rock in which the stream we had crossed had been swallowed up. There was no point even in waiting for each other: impossible to exchange a word, to approach each other without turning aside and taking longer steps. This paradoxical situation became worse and worse until the immediate surroundings of a little deserted fort, around which we walked, each on our side, but this time I was near the sea. Suddenly my unease reached its peak when I discovered in the enclosure of this fort two or three men who had stopped mowing a ridiculously small square of field to take turns watching us.

I hasten to say that, once this fort was left behind and cut off from our sight by a new outcrop of rock, a progressive clearing was produced outside as well as within us. A very long and smooth beach stretched its harmonious curve between the sea and the sky; roofs and treetops were visible. Nothing but deplorable pride could have required, for its satisfaction, that we each persisted for a bit in our attitude. After which we had no trouble in agreeing that the torment we had just undergone was founded on nothing which, in reality, imperiled our love. Insofar as we had been led to despair of each other for a while, we could only have been under the sway of some delirium.

Back in Lorient at my parents' house, I told them how we had spent these last hours, omitting, of course, what had been so disturbing. To my great surprise, the conversation took no time in heating up: really, we had gone that near the "villa of the Loch," *the house of Michel Henriot?* There was no possible doubt from the details given me: this house was the one I had perceived in a fog only my own, surrounded by the worst kind of wasteland. And the whole criminal case reconstituted itself under my eyes, one of the most singular, the most picturesque cases imaginable. It had indeed in its time occasioned much discussion, but I had not thought of it at all since then, and it was impossible for me to unearth the slightest association of ideas that might have persuaded me to think of it again recently. Moreover, the exterior appearance of this house, even with the *aura* I had found myself attributing to it, is so everyday that you could not possibly recognize it from the pictures published in the papers.

Here I open a parenthesis to declare that contrary to the current interpretation, I think Cézanne is not above all a painter of apples,

but the painter of *The House of the Hanged Man.* I insist that the technical preoccupations, which everyone starts to talk about as soon as it is a question of Cézanne, make us too systematically forget the concern he showed, on several occasions, to treat these subjects having an *aura,* from ever since *The Murder* of 1870, which bears witness to this concern with evidence, up to the *Players* of 1892, around which there floats a half-tragic, half-guignolesque menace in every point resembling the one pictured in the card game of Chaplin's film *A Dog's Life,* together with the *Young Man before a Skull* of 1890, in its apparent conception of an ultraconventional romanticism, but in its execution extending far beyond this romanticism: metaphysical unease falls on the painting *through the pleats of the curtain. The House of the Hanged Man,* in particular, has always seemed to me very singularly placed on the canvas of 1885, placed so as to render an account of something else entirely than its exterior aspect as a house, at least to present it under its most suspicious angle: the horizontal black patch above the window, the crumbling, towards the left, of the wall on the first level. This is not just anecdotal: it is a question, painting, for example, of the necessity of expressing the relationship which cannot fail to exist between the fall of a human body, a cord strung around its neck, into emptiness, and the place itself where this drama has come to pass, a place which it is, moreover, human nature to come and inspect. Consciousness of this relation for Cézanne suffices to explain to me why he pushed the building back on the right in such a way as to hide it in part and, after that, to make it appear *higher.* I willingly admit that, because of his particular aptitude to perceive these auras and to concentrate his attention on them, Cézanne was led to study them in their immediacy, considering them in their most elementary structure. Such an aura exists, just as well, around an apple, even if it is only constituted by the desire it might arouse to eat it. Everything comes down, in the final analysis, to taking account of the relations of light which, from the point of view of knowledge, should perhaps be considered in its very simplest details. In any case, as these relations are more or less fitting, they will determine the greater or lesser intensity of sensation. It all happens as if one were in the presence of a phenomenon of particular refraction where the nontransparent medium is constituted by the human mind. The principle of this phenomenon must always be the same, and in order to pinpoint it, we might think it better to stand hypnotized before an Iceland spar than to try to take immediate account of a mirage. It is nonetheless true that on several occasions Cézanne felt he needed to confront the most troublesome aspects of such a problem.

They reminded me of the details of the Loch affair: a young woman killed by a hunting rifle in this house I had glimpsed; her husband, Michel Henriot, the son of the attorney general of Lorient, testifying that the murder had taken place in his absence and probably should be attributed to some tramp, as had been many other recent crimes not yet solved. The dangerous isolation of the house, which he had built a little after his marriage, was to be explained by the fact that he raised *silver foxes* in the outlying buildings. Then the inquiry established that he had, shortly after that, drawn up an insurance contract for his own benefit in case his wife should predecease him, this insurance formally taking into account the risk of murder, and that, the next morning after the crime, Attorney Henriot had asked on the telephone that the insurance company involved begin its assessment. "All Lorient," it seemed, had gone to the funeral, whose first part followed the same trajectory we had. The crowd, during the whole procession behind the Henriots, had been of the most unruly sort, the son trying to hide his *fox's* profile behind some stereotyped words of regret, the father very dignified in face of the uproar (he was reputed for his severity, which had earned him the nickname of the Attorney Maximum: people said, in fact, that when it was a matter of moderate sentences on the part of his representatives, he had always intervened personally to ask for the maximum penalty). The interrogation of Michel Henriot had started up again, leading rather quickly to confession: he had killed her, but he denied any self-interested motivation. If one were to believe him, he had obeyed the exasperation caused by his wife's long-standing refusal to give in to his sexual advances, a refusal again inflicted on him that very day. Besides these specifics, which the legal investigation had to be satisfied with or not, there was naturally a whole series of investigations which never got very far, chiefly because a psychoanalytic examination had not been carried out. But these investigations, almost left to chance, had nevertheless furnished a few interesting details having to do with the personality of the criminal: a neurotic heredity on the mother's side—she loved to shoot, and her extreme attachment to her child had contrasted utterly with the professional indifference and the impassivity of the father. The son was of a sickly complexion and of a great intellectual mediocrity not exempt from oddness (his late choice of the fox-raising profession being typical). The more than hasty arrangement of the marriage, through newspaper ads, removed in his mind any necessity of preliminaries, any need to see if there were affinities; it reflected in every way, and solely, the sordid desire of the parents to see the match, not of two beings, but of two fortunes. Letters from Madame Michel Henriot to her sister were read aloud, letters in which, showing no illusion about the fate awaiting her, she asked for help without managing to have anyone worry about her at all. A lovely testimony in honor of the bourgeois family.

But that evening I was too preoccupied by some apparently "poetic" aspects of the question, to let myself reflect at length on these moral considerations. I remembered some articles reporting the testimony of several witnesses to the fact that Michel Henriot used to shoot seabirds for pleasure, and I saw myself a few hours earlier putting these same birds to flight by throwing stones at them. The fact is that for the first time, and in that place, their behavior had been disagreeable to me. An illustrated history of France, probably the first that I ever saw, around the age of four, showed a very young King Louis XV massacring some birds in an aviary in that way, *just for his pleasure.* I do not know whether I had already discovered cruelty then, but there is no doubt that I retain, in relation to that image, a certain ambivalence in feeling. The silver foxes also set me to wondering: were they numerous, how did they adjust to the climate? One detail: whether it is irritating or heavily ironic, I cannot decide. I learned that, as soon as Henriot was arrested, the Society for the Prevention of Cruelty to Animals had written to ask that they be allowed to take care of the foxes.

Above all I could not detach myself from another detail, of the greatest subjective importance for me: the little fort that I had found myself in front of after crossing the stream was no other, they assured me, than the provisional dwelling that Michel Henriot and his wife had chosen during the time that it took to construct for them the "villa of the Loch." Thus the space between these two buildings, which had been for me that afternoon such an exceptional place of disgrace, revealed itself, *in its very limits,* to be the previous theatre of a singular tragedy. Everything had occurred as if I had undergone, as if I had not been alone in undergoing, precisely from one to the other, the effects of deleterious emanations attacking the very principle of moral life. Should we admit that the curse had fallen on this place after the crime, or see, already in the crime itself, the accomplishment of that curse? This question remained, naturally, without an answer. It could have been elucidated only by undertaking in that place itself research on the oldest memories attached to that strip of land. This research would have been long, arduous, and probably of little consequence. And in addition, the real problem, so far as I saw it, had always been something else: Is the mirror of love between two beings likely to be clouded over by the very fact of circumstances totally foreign to love and to be unclouded, suddenly, when these circumstances cease? Yes.

I cannot pretend not to know how medieval such a way of seeing, in the eyes of certain positivistic minds, may seem. How will it look when I add that at this precise spot in my reflections a blazing streak crossed my mind! This streak—how shall I put it?—was not a streak of light because even at a distance it does not permit me to understand, to profit fully from what it made me *see:* on the eve of our departure, my wife having asked one of our friends to lend her for these few days something light to read, the friend had brought her two English novels: *The Fox,* by Mary Webb, and *The Woman Changed into a Fox,* by David Garnett. I had been struck, in that moment, by the analogy of these two titles (our friend, making a hasty choice in his library, must not have remembered which of these corresponded to the content that he liked). Also remarkable, I had known the second of these works for a long time, and I had enjoyed rereading it in the days before this. This July 20 in particular, the two volumes and just they alone were in our room, within easy reach on little tables *on either side* of the bed.

Like it or not, we have to recognize that these two books seem, in the elaboration of what was for us this long waking nightmare, to have played an *overdetermining* and decisive role. Through what mystery did they manage to enter into the composition with the other elements such as this house, this stream—the Loch itself—

this fort (which none of us could identify), provoking in us simultaneously an affective state *in total contradiction* to our real feelings? Why, very precisely, had these two books accompanied us to Brittany? Everything happens as if, in such a case, one were the victim of a learned machination on the part of powers which remain, until things change, highly obscure. If we want to avoid this machination's involving, by a simple confusion of levels, a lasting unrest in love or at least a grave doubt about its continuing, we are faced with the necessity of *undoing* it.

I insisted, some days later, on confronting the memory I had retained of this malevolent place with reality. . . To my very great surprise, the enclosure that had contained the foxes was closed, not, as I had thought I saw it the first day, by a metallic trellis, but by a cement wall too high to permit me to see what was on the inside. Standing on the seats of their cars, people who had obviously driven here for that purpose seemed to be more fortunate. Seen close up, the house was not at all different from the image I had kept of it, except that at the window of the first floor there were three women, Parisian in bearing, rather pretty. On the door of the pen, in white letters on a black background, I read: "Change of ownership. No trespassing." After some gymnastic effort, I managed to see that all the cages, *with metallic trellises,* were leaned against the wall which had been facing me first. It was as if, on July 20, this wall had been *transparent* for me. The yellow stream was the same. An engraved plaque restricted itself to the evocation of the fort's activity: "Fort du Loch 1746–1862."

7 Dear Hazel of Squirrelnut,[1]
In the lovely springtime of 1952 you will just be sixteen, and perhaps you will be tempted to open this book, whose title, I like to think,

will be wafted to you euphonically by the wind bending the hawthorns. . . All possible dreams, hopes, and illusions will dance, I hope, night and day, illuminated by your curls, and I shall doubtless be there no longer; I would have liked to be there just to see you. Mysterious, resplendent horsemen will dash by at dusk, beside the changeable streams. Garbed in light sea-green veils, a young girl will glide sleepwalking under high archways, where a single votive lamp will flicker. But the spirits of the reeds, the tiny cats seeming to sleep in the rings, the elegant toy pistol perforated with the word "Ball," will keep you from taking these scenes tragically. Whatever your lot will be, increasingly fortunate or entirely other, I cannot know, you will delight in living, expecting everything from love. Whatever happens from now until you read this letter—it seems that what we least expect is what will come to pass—let me believe you will be ready then to incarnate this eternal power of woman, the only power I have ever submitted to. Whether you have just closed a school desk on a world crow-blue in high fantasy, or whether your sunny silhouette, except for the bouquet of flowers on your blouse, is cast against the wall of a factory—I am far from sure about your future—let me believe that these words, "mad love," will one day correspond uniquely to your own delirium.

They will not keep their promise because they will only enlighten for you the mystery of your birth. For a long time I thought it was the gravest insanity to give life. In any case I held it against those who had given it to me. It may be that you would hold it against me on some days. That is in fact why I have chosen to see you at sixteen, when you cannot hold it against me. What am I saying, to look at you, no, rather to try to see through your eyes, to look at myself through your eyes.

My little child, just eight months old, always smiling, made at once like coral and like pearls, you will know then that any element of chance was strictly excluded from your coming, that your birth came about at the exact time that it was supposed to, neither sooner nor later, and that no shadow was awaiting you above your wicker cradle. Even that great poverty which had been and remains mine let up for a few days. I was not, as it happens, opposed to this poverty: I accepted to pay the price for not being a slave to life, to settle for the right I had assumed once and for all to not express any ideas but my own. We were not many in doing this. . . Poverty passed by in the distance, made lovelier and almost justified, a little like what has been called, in the case of a painter who was one of your first friends, *the blue period*.[2] It seemed the almost inevitable consequence of my refusal to behave the way almost all the others did, whether on one side or on another. This poverty, whether you have had the time to dread it or not, imagine it was only the other side of the miraculous coin of your existence: the Night of the Sunflower would have been less radiant without it.

Less radiant because then love would not have had to confront all it did confront, because it would not have had, in order to triumph, to count in everything and for everything on itself only. Perhaps this was a terrible imprudence, but it was exactly this imprudence that was the loveliest jewel of the case. Beyond this imprudence there remained nothing except an even greater one: that of bringing you to life, whose perfumed breath you are. It was necessary, at least, to extend from one to the other a magic cord, stretched to the breaking point above the precipice so that beauty could rise, with just its balancing rod, to pluck you like an impossible flower of the air. May you delight at least one day in believing you are this flower, that you were born with no contact with the ground, unfortunately unsterile as it is with what is commonly called "human affairs." You have come from the slightest shimmer of what was rather late for me the goal of poetry, to which I have been devoted since my youth, of that poetry I continue now to serve, scorning everything else. You appeared there as if by magic, and if ever you detect a trace of sadness in these words that for the first time I address *to you alone,* say to yourself that this enchantment continues and will continue to be identified with you, that it is strong enough to rise above any heartbreak. *Forever,* and *for a long time* – those two great warring expressions that confront each other whenever it is a question of love – have never exchanged more blinding sword-thrusts than today, above me, in a sky entirely like your eyes, whose whites are still so blue. Of these two expressions, the one that wears my colors, even if its star may be waning now, even if it must lose, is *forever. Forever,* as in the oaths that girls insist on hearing. *Forever,* as on the white sand of time and through the grace of this instrument which is used to measure it, but only fascinates you and leaves you hungry, reduced to a stream of milk endlessly pouring from a glass breast. Despite everything, I shall have maintained that this expression *forever* is the master key. What I have loved, whether I have kept it or not, I shall love *forever.* As you are called upon to suffer also, I wanted, in completing this book, to explain to you. I have spoken of a certain "sublime point" on the mountain. It was never a question of establishing my dwelling on this point. It would, moreover, from then on, have ceased to be sublime and I should, myself, have ceased to be a person. Unable reasonably to dwell there, I have nevertheless never gone so far from it as to lose it from view, as to not be able to point it out. I had chosen to be this guide, and therefore I had forced myself not to be unworthy of the power which, in the direction of eternal love, had made me *see* and granted me the still rarer privilege of *having others see.* I have never been unworthy; I have never ceased to identify the flesh of the being I love and the snow of the peaks in the rising

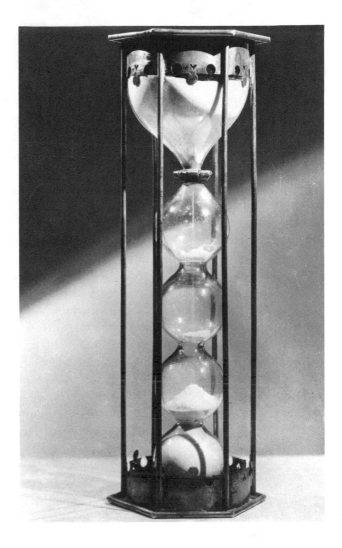

*A stream of milk endlessly pouring
from a glass breast* (p.114)
Photograph by Man Ray.
© A.D.A.G.P., Paris
V.A.G.A., New York 1986

sun. I have tried only to know the hours of love's triumph, whose necklace I here clasp about your throat. Even the black pearl, the last one, I am sure you will understand what weakness attaches me to it, what supreme hope of *conjuration* I have placed on it. I do not deny that love has a difference with life. I say it should vanquish, and in order to do so, should rise to such a poetic consciousness of itself that every hostile thing it meets should melt in the hearth of its own splendor.

At least that will have been, permanently, my great hope, un-diminished by my not always being able to show myself worthy. If it ever mingles with another hope, I am sure this latter is just as important for you. I have wanted your existence to know for itself this *raison d'être,* that I had asked it of what was for me beauty, in all the fullest strength of the term, love, in all the strength of the term; the name I give you at the top of this letter does not just render, in its anagrammatical form, a charming account of your *present* aspect, because, after having invented it for you, I perceived that I had originally used the words that make it up to characterize the very aspect that *love* had taken for me: this must be what *resemblance* is. I also wanted everything that I expect from human becoming, everything that, as I see it, is worth fighting for collectively and not just individually, to cease being a formal manner of thinking, even the noblest, to confront this reality of life becoming that you are. I mean that at one time in my life I feared being cut off from the necessary contact, from the human contact with what would be after me. *After me:* this idea keeps getting lost but turns up again wonderfully in a certain sleight of hand that you have, *like* (and for me not like) all little children. From the very first day, I admired your hand. It hovered about everything intellectual I had tried to construct, as if to render it inane. What a mad thing this hand is, and how I pity those who have never had the chance to place it, like a star, on the loveliest page of a book. The poverty, suddenly, of any flower. We only have to look at this hand to think that any human makes a deplorable account of what he thinks he knows. All he understands from it is that it is really made, in all senses, for the *best*. This blind aspiration towards the best would suffice to justify love as I think of it, absolute love, as the only principle for physical and moral selection which can guarantee that human witness, human passage shall not have taken place in vain.

I was thinking of all this, feverishly, in September 1936, alone with you in my famous, unlivable house of rock salt. I was thinking about it between reading newspapers telling, more or less hypocritically, the episodes of the Civil War in Spain, the newspapers behind which you thought I was disappearing just to play peek-a-boo with you. And it was also true, because in such moments, the unconscious and the conscious, in you and in me, existed in complete duality near each other, keeping each other in a total ignorance and yet communicating at will by a single all-powerful thread which was the exchanged glance between us. To be sure, my life then hung only by the slightest thread. Great was the temptation to go offer it to those who, without any possible error and any distinction of tendencies, wanted at any price to finish with the old "order" founded on the cult of that abject trinity: family, country, and religion. And still you held me by that thread which is happiness, such as it pierces the web of unhappiness itself. I loved in you all the little children of the Spanish militia, like those I had seen running naked in the outer district of Santa Cruz, on Tenerife. May the sacrifice of so many human lives make of them one day *happy* beings! And yet I did not feel in myself the courage to expose you with me to help that to happen.

All the little children of the Spanish militia . . . (p.117)
Photograph by Henri Cartier-Bresson

Above all, let the idea of the family be buried! If I have loved in you the working out of natural necessity, it is to the exact extent that in your person it was one with what was for me human necessity, *logical* necessity; the reconciliation of these two necessities has always seemed to me the only miracle within the reach of any human, the only chance of escaping now and then the meanness of the human condition. You have gone from nonbeing to being by one of these agreements which are the only ones to which I cared to listen. You were thought of as possible, as certain, in the very moment when, in a love deeply sure of itself, a man and a woman wanted you to be.

I wanted you too much to hear you one day answering in complete innocence those insidious questions grownups ask children: "What do we think with, suffer with? How did we get the sun's name? Where does the night come from?" As if they could answer the questions themselves! Since you are for me the human creature in its perfect authenticity, you should, improbable as it seems, teach me about them. . .

I want you to be madly loved.

Notes

TRANSLATOR'S INTRODUCTION

1. Breton's major works: *Clair de terre,* Collection Littérature (Paris: Galli-mard, 1923); *Le Surréalisme et la peinture,* NRF (Paris: Gallimard, 1928); *Nadja,* NRF (Paris: Gallimard, 1928); *Les Vases communicants* (Editions des Cahiers Libres, 1932); *L'Amour fou,* NRF (Paris: Gallimard, 1937); *Arcane 17* (New York: Editions Brentano's, 1945).

2. See descriptions in *Les Pas perdus* (Paris: Gallimard, 1923). The title refers to the Hall of the Wasted Steps (la Salle des Pas perdus) in railway stations, and also carries the meaning of the Not-Lost or Not-Wasted.

3. We could read also (and many have) *Lits et ratures* ("Beds and erasures").

4. *Poems of André Breton,* ed. and trans. Jean-Pierre Cauvin and Mary Ann Caws (Austin: University of Texas Press, 1983).

5. One of Braque's concerns, quoted by Breton in *Le Surréalisme et la peinture.*

6. Courtly love, as illustrated in medieval romance and just after, is part of the surrealist tradition of the irrational.

7. Yves Bonnefoy suggested this convincing idea to me in conversation.

8. See the Péret chapter in my *Poetry of Dada and Surrealism* (Princeton: Princeton University Press, 1971).

9. For an analysis of how the surrealist image works, in relation to *Mad Love* and also to other texts, see in particular Rosalind E. Krauss's "The Uses of Surrealist Photography," in her *The Originality of the Avant-Garde and Other Modernist Myths* (Cambridge: MIT Press, 1985), and Rosalind E. Krauss and Jane Livingston, *L'Amour fou: Surrealism and Photography* (New York: Abbeville Press, 1985).

10. *Difference in Translation,* ed. Joseph Graham (Ithaca: Cornell University Press, 1985).

SECTION I

1. "*Boys*" appears in English in the original. To begin such an unfamiliar word and to italicize it is already to make a frontal attack on the separation of the natural and the artificial as we conceive of them. For an interesting illustration of Breton's relation to his own showmanship, see the poem "Rideau, rideau" ("Curtain, curtain"), in which he variously plays the roles of spectator, actor, prompter, assassin, and victim:

> The vagabond theatres of the seasons which will have
>   played out my life
> Under my catcalls
> The forestage had been set up as a cell from which
>   I could hiss
>
> .   .   .   .
>
> A character moved about the hall the only agile one
> Who had made himself a mask with my features
> He viciously sided with the ingenue and the traitor
>
> .   .   .   .
>
> The basement was marvelous there appeared on a white
>   wall my silhouette fire-specked

2. Instead of "pursuing me with their dart or arrow," Breton uses the wonderful baroque formulation of the trace or mark left by the dart

or arrow as that which does the pursuing. This is an excellent example of the elliptical style complicating the original, to say nothing of obscuring the translated version: I have chosen to leave it "marked," that is, and paradoxically intact.

3. Alfred Jarry is best known for *Ubu roi,* a play written when he was fifteen. Jarry's *Haldernablou* (1894), written when he was twenty-one, is already in its title a coupling of two names: that of the Duke Haldern and that of his page Ablou, whom he loves, possesses, and eventually loathes. It is always a text of doubling and redoubling, of people, emotions, objects; the desire for androgyny is strong in each self represented ("the double beast coupled"). At the time of Jarry's homosexual involvement with Leon-Paul Fargue (one of the keys to the text), they were reading Lautréamont's *Chants de Maldoror* together, and its influence is clearly marked in the desperate sadism. Most striking of all is the presence of the one-eyed skull, on which Haldern meditates at length until a similar one opens up inside his own head.

4. Cinderella (and her originating ashes) will reappear.

5. Ashes and snow are a perfect surrealist oxymoron, including the clash of heat and cold, dark and light.

6. "Que salubre est le vent!" from "La Rivière à Cassis," in *Rimbaud: Oeuvres Poétiques* (Paris: Garnier Flammarion, 1984), p. 96.

7. "La nuit vieillissait," from Mallarmé's translation of Poe's poem "Ulalume," in *Oeuvres complètes de Stéphane Mallarmé,* Pléiade ed. (Paris: Gallimard, 1945), p. 197.

8. Paul Valéry was a great influence on Breton in the latter's symbolist period, as were Arthur Rimbaud, Stéphane Mallarmé, and Edgar Allan Poe; Pierre Louys was a florid and wonderfully decadent postsymbolist.

9. Isidore Ducasse, comte de Lautréamont, one of the surrealist heroes, is responsible for the most celebrated encounter of all surrealism: "Beautiful as the encounter of a sewing machine with an umbrella on a dissection table. . . ."

10. Justine and Juliette are creations of the Marquis de Sade, in volumes named for them; Matthew Gregory Lewis's *The Monk* (1795) was one of the highlights of the Gothic tales or "black novels" the surrealists fancied.

11. Charles Baudelaire's own *Flowers of Evil* did indeed hold Breton in their sway (and surrealist oxymoronic imagination in their technique); Charles Cros and Germain Nouveau were minor symbolist writers; Jacques Vaché, responsible for UMOUR, without the *H* of "Humour," committed his final humorous act by overdosing with drugs and taking two friends along with him in a triple suicide; Guillaume Apollinaire is the great Cubist writer; we might as well forget Michel Féline, since we are told to.

12. Convulsive beauty is linked to the conventions of hysterical neurotic patients (Breton worked in a psychiatric ward) and to the meeting of opposites. As cubism can be thought to be the picturing of an object many times from many angles of repose, and futurism to be the picturing of it in action, surrealism combines the two tendencies.

13. This picture is all the stronger for not being pictured.

14. This celebrated "éloge du cristal" is in a sense emblematic of the whole surrealist morality and Breton's own high conception of it.

15. Work, said the surrealists, is a German concept; spontaneity, a French one.

16. Hegel's figures, like his dialectic, haunt Breton's thought and, in particular, his visual imagination as it connects with his esthetic theory. For example, he delights in the way in which Hegel brings the sense of detailed metaphor to the surface, making clear the relation of the "figure" focussed on as it stands out in relief against the "ground." Art object or object in nature, these two combine, in surrealism, in another form of the dialectic, bypassing and resuming all antinomies, whether conceived of spiritually in concept or in material appearance, as illustrated in this material rendering of the spirit. Breton quotes

Hegel, then: "The art object lies midway between the tangible and the rational. It is a spiritual thing that appears material. Insofar as they address themselves to the imagination and the senses, art and poetry purposely create a world of shadows, of phantoms, of fictive images; and yet one cannot accuse them of being incapable of producing anything other than forms empty of all reality." Breton, *Position politique du surréalisme* (Paris: Sagittaire, 1935), p. 122.

17. *L'objet trouvé* is of course the *trouvaille*, the thing found and always turned towards the positive, seeming at once surprising and necessary.

18. Breton is referring, of course, to Charles Baudelaire's sonnet called "Correspondances," with its famous lines

> La Nature est un temple où de vivant piliers
> Laissent parfois sortir de confuses paroles;
> L'homme y passe à travers des forêts de symboles
> Qui l'observent avec des regards familiers.

This can be roughly rendered as "Nature is a temple where living pillars / Sometimes emit confused words; / Man goes through forests of symbols / That watch him with intimate looks." Baudelaire, *Les Fleurs du mal*, Bibliothèque de Cluny (Paris: Armand Colin, 1958), p. 11.

SECTION 2

1. In the French, *sur une lapalissade de haut goût*. In honor of the patron of the French truism, La Palisse (1470–1525), an example:

> M. de La Palisse est mort
> il est mort de maladie
> 1/4 d'heure avant sa mort
> il était toujours en vie.

(M. de La Palisse is dead / he is dead of sickness / a quarter of an hour before he died / he was still alive.)

2. "Progressively adjust to" translates *accommodation progressive à* – as the eye, after darkness, becomes used to light. The best description of the *encounter* as surrealism knew it is to be found in *Les Vases communicants* (Paris: Gallimard, 1955), pp. 130ff. (the episode of the Café Batifol).

SECTION 3

1. *L'attente:* the state of waiting, of expectation, akin to André Gide's state of readiness, of the *disponibilité* Breton has just mentioned two sentences before. The readiness for an undefined event, in all its openness, permits the advent of the marvelous.

2. André Breton, *Nadja* (Paris: Gallimard, 1963), pp. 49–50, on the Flea Market of Saint-Ouen: "I go there often, looking for those objects not to be found anywhere else, out of fashion, in bits and pieces, useless, almost incomprehensible, really perverse in the sense I mean and love."

3. The found object, or the *trouvaille* (see n. 17 to section I, above), is invested with the sense of the marvelous, as one "hits on something."

4. Cf. *Les Vases communicants* (Denoël et Steele). [Breton's note.]

5. *Phrase de réveil* ("waking sentence"): the sentence that taps on the window, as it was originally described by Breton; *le Cendrier Cendrillon:* cendres/cinders, a surrealist word play.

6. *Du mot "vair":* the words *verre* ("glass") and *vair* ("ermine fur," but also "variable") sound exactly alike. I have played instead on glass.

7. Cf. *La Révolution surréaliste,* March 1928; *Variétés,* June 1929. [Breton's note.]

8. Giacometti: "What is violet?" Breton: "It's a double fly." Breton: "What is art?" Giacometti: "It's a white shell in a basin of water." Etc. [Breton's note.]

9. See note 6, above.

10. Freud, *Essais de psychanalyse* (Payot ed.): "Le moi et le soi." [Breton's note.]

1. See *Nadja* (NRF ed.), *Les Vases communicants* (Denoël et Steele ed.). [Breton's note.]

2. For Hegel, and the relation of the spiritual to the object world of the material and the natural, see note 16 to section I. Hegel is everywhere in Breton: in the passage about the crystal in *Mad Love;* in *The Communicating Vessels,* where Hegel's recollection of Napoleon is quoted when Napoleon questions, in the "ideological class" he visits, the relation between waking and dream (*Les Vases communicants,* pp. 178–80).

3. *Le plus merveilleux chemin des écoliers:* marvelous to the school children because it is the longest path.

4. See *Le Revolver à cheveux blancs* (Denoël et Steele ed.). [Breton's note.]

5. *Tourne, sol:* while creating the sensation of dizziness ("turn, earth"), this expression is also a play on the sunflower (*tournesol*), which turns toward the sun (*soleil*), thus containing verbally the earth (*sol*).

6. See *Point du jour* (NRF ed.), "Le Message Automatique." [Breton's note.]

7. *Earth Light* is an example of reciprocal illumination of one term by the other.

8. The play is on *survenants,* or the chance comers, and *revenants,* or the returning ghosts.

9. Adapted from Caws and Cauvin, *Poems of André Breton* (Austin: University of Texas Press, 1983).

10. The Square of the Innocents in Paris (named for the Massacre of the Innocents), where the twelfth-century church was destroyed in 1786, contains a restored fountain of Pierre Lescot and Jean Goujon (1550).

11. See Breton's poem about the Lying-In Hospital, and about giving birth, "It was about to be five in the morning."

12. *Les Chants de Maldoror,* sixth canto. [Breton's note.]

13. René Char and Paul Eluard were Breton's good friends, surrealists both for a while; then Char left the movement for his own direction, and Eluard, for political reasons.

14. "Clé de sol" is a musical key (G), and "Tournesol" the sunflower. The formal echo and the bringing into play of additional meanings adds to the baroque flavor of Breton's highly figural and enormously complex textuality, as *sol*, "ground," *sol* the musical key, and *sol* half of the sun (*soleil*) all spin around in the reader's imagination like the sunflower turning to the sun.

15. *Pierre:* stone; *reverdy:* to become green again, or to take on a greenish cast. Thus, a stone that does gather moss.

16. On Jacques Vaché, see note 11 to section I, above.

SECTION 5

1. *A la barbe de Barbebleue:* literally, in the beard (in the face) of Bluebeard, despite him, or to flaunt him.

2. No longer the only, but one of the two only ones since that other prodigious film, the triumph of surrealist thought, *Peter Ibbettson*. [Breton's note.]

3. In the French, the preposition is *à*, as in *arbre à pain, arbre à beurre*, translated ordinarily as "bread tree," etc., were there not already a (different) bread tree.

4. *Virginies:* the conflation of two meanings—Virginia, as in the Deep South, and also Paul et Virginie, the latter being the modest heroine who was too shy to remove her clothes and who therefore drowned in her modesty.

5. Breton is referring to Rimbaud's "La Bonne Auberge."

6. *La sensitive:* otherwise known as *mimosa pudica*. The link with the Virginias above is clear, in their double southern climate.

7. *Un écran:* both a screen and a grid, against which and through which we are to read the clues and ourselves.

8. Translation from Richard Howard, *Les Fleurs du mal* (Boston: Godine, 1982), p. 154. The cities have not made their appearance in the translation, but nothing of Baudelaire is lost.

9. The *déjà vu,* familiar in psychology, is here taken literally, and creates its opposition, the *jamais vu,* the virginal sight.

SECTION 7

1. *Chère Ecusette de Noireuil:* a double switch between the words *écureuil,* or squirrel, and *noisette,* or hazelnut; I have contented myself with one-half of the play.
2. Picasso's blue periods are the referent here.